AT THE

EDGE

OF ALL

THINGS

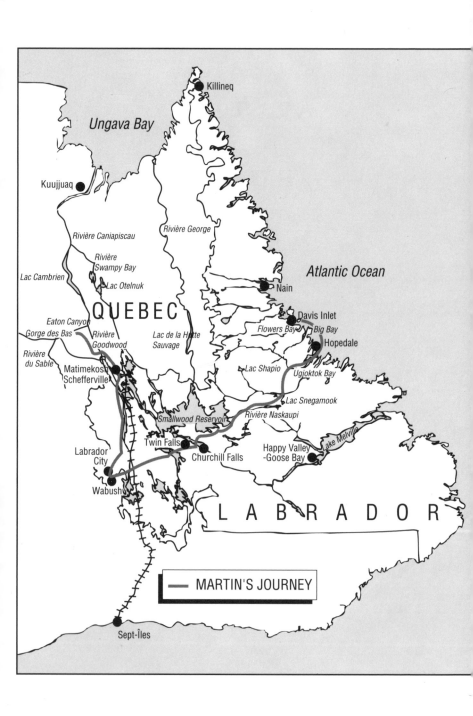

Killineq

Ungava Bay

Kuujjuaq

Rivière Caniapiscau

Rivière George

*Rivière
Swampy Bay*

Lac Cambrien

Lac Otelnuk

Atlantic Ocean

QUEBEC

Nain

Eaton Canyon
Gorge des Bas

Davis Inlet

*Rivière
Goodwood*

*Lac de la Hutte
Sauvage*

Flowers Bay Big Bay

Hopedale

*Rivière
du Sable*

Matimekosh
Schefferville

Lac Shapio

Ugjoktok Bay

Lac Snegamook

Smallwood Reservoir

Rivière Naskaupi

Twin Falls

Labrador
City

Churchill Falls

Happy Valley
-Goose Bay

Lake Melville

Wabush

LABRADOR

MARTIN'S JOURNEY

Sept-Îles

AT THE

EDGE

OF ALL

THINGS

In Search of Labrador

RICK HORNUNG

Published in 1995 by
Stoddart Publishing Co. Limited
34 Lesmill Road
Toronto, Canada
M3B 2T6
Tel. (416) 445-3333
Fax (416) 445-5967

Stoddart Books are available for bulk purchase for
sales promotions, premiums, fundraising, and seminars.
For details, contact the **Special Sales Department** at
the above address.

Canadian Cataloguing in Publication Data

Hornung, Rick
At the edge of all things : in search of Labrador

ISBN 0-7737-2859-7

1. Labrador (Nfld.).   2. Rouleau, Martin.
3. Labrador (Nfld.) - Description and travel.
I. Title.

FC2193.4.H67 1994   971.8`204   C95-930055-4
F1140.H67 1994

Cover Design: Bill Douglas/The Bang
Typesetting: Tony Gordon
Printed and bound in Canada

Names of the men and women in this book have
been changed to protect their identities.

*Stoddart Publishing gratefully acknowledges the support
of the Canada Council, the Ontario Ministry of Culture,
Tourism, and Recreation, Ontario Arts Council, and
Ontario Publishing Centre in the development of
writing and publishing in Canada.*

To Sarah,
who brings laughter into our house
and to Gabriel,
who blows the blues away

CONTENTS

PROLOGUE

I awaken in the earliest hours of morning and roll from my back onto my left side. Now I can look out the window and watch the blue-black glimmers of night fade to the indigo-tipped sky that slips through the oak branches. I used to have trouble falling asleep and trouble waking up — tossing and turning, then sliding into a deep slumber broken only by an alarm clock or bursts of daylight crossing my bed. But now an unsettled sleep jumps over me, the dreams becoming fragments of memories that jar my eyes open and leave me staring at the predawn sky.

This morning I'm whizzing into Davis Inlet. The sun has already begun its swing to the south, glazing the snow on Ukasikalik Island. The path is clear, Sango Bay lies due west, beyond the iced bumps that form Flat Island, Duck Rock, and Pigeon Island. On my right, there's a dogleg.

Due north, swerve left.

I'm on a snowmobile with a hunter in search of caribou. Each of our machines pulls a twelve-foot sled, his carrying fuel, food, a tent, a stove, a chain saw; mine has the sleeping bags, axes, cross-country skis. The rest of the space is cleared for the animals we might kill. At thirty-five kilometres an hour, morning has buzzed into afternoon.

There's nothing but the sound of our engines. I'm going too fast to tell the difference between one rock and another. My eyes are watering, the liquid freezing to the foam padding of my goggles, turning its spongelike texture into a block.

But I'm not cold, just scared. I'm afraid the rifle on my back may go off and I won't hear it above the torque of the machines.

Taking a left and accelerating, I think about a bullet beneath my shoulder blade.

That's when I wake up.

When I first considered a trip to Labrador at the end of 1991, I was an investigative reporter working for a New York newspaper. I'd read a brief dispatch about the Innu of Davis Inlet competing with their northern neighbours, the Inuit, over land and mineral rights. A bit of digging at the library uncovered what appeared to be a long, tumultuous history of aboriginals and invaders fighting one another and amongst themselves to determine borders, ownership of resources, religious affiliations, government jurisdictions. A fact sheet from the Canadian consulate explained that centuries of conflict involved the governments of Newfoundland, Quebec, Canada, France and England, Portugal and Spain.

I can still see myself in the reading room that overlooks Fifth Avenue, the reference books spread out across the mahogany table, photocopies of newspaper and magazine articles arranged in a semicircle, my body rocking back the wooden chair. I have a photography book on my lap, and I'm checking out the pictures of streams and lakes, ice and cliffs, a village nestled between the rocks. Perhaps, I thought, it was time to get out of New York and change my rhythm.

The maps, the flight routes, the rails, the river, and sea passages seemed so clear: start at the Lachine rapids and follow the St. Lawrence; start at Jacques Cartier's point of discovery and retrace his steps; start at the entrance to Iroquoia and journey northeast through the Algonkian lands; start at Dorval and jet to the military base at Goose Bay; drive along the Côte du Nord to Sept-Îles, then take the train to Schefferville. There was a simple logic, a series of straight lines joining precise points, a mathematical certainty that led me to see a region that could be divided into identifiable parts coming together to form a peninsula.

I organized files and folders, bibliographies, computerized reference materials, geological texts, mineralogical data. There was a list of phone numbers — tourist offices, hotels, outfitters and hunting guides, charter aircraft operators, fishermen and boats for hire.

I made notes and began diaries, arranged for special privileges in research libraries in Ottawa, Montreal, Toronto, St. John's, Quebec, a string of universities and seminaries, the Smithsonian Institution, and geographical societies that sponsored turn-of-the-century expeditions to a land where no white man had penetrated.

When the death of six children in a Valentine's Day fire in the Labrador peninsula drew international attention in 1992, my editors said it was time to go. Now there was a story to tell.

After the first few days, I realized there was more to the story than gathering obscure facts and outhustling reporters determined to chronicle the tale of neglect, substance abuse, Innu despair, and white domination. Though it was right to map the colonial exploitation and bureaucratic deceit that led to the conditions that created the fire, this path did not fully explain the conflicting and contradictory choices made by individuals who refused to leave the peninsula.

Beyond the airstrips and band-council offices, I found a network of smugglers and grifters, hustlers and hunters, caught between the harsh political realities of contemporary Canada and the timeless challenge of Labrador's terrain. These men and women took the irregular pieces of geography and created a political economy and a social history. That was my story. Instead of examining the front-page disputes over iron-ore mines, fisheries, land rights, social-service grants, mineral rights, NATO bases, and radar installations, I travelled the bizarre underground of men and women who worked a series of black markets to earn the cash needed for essentials.

It took more than two years to understand what I saw and

heard. Veering off to the west, backtracking to the south to examine Quebec City and the Saguenay, punching north, then suddenly jumping to the Atlantic coast, hitching a ride to Pointe Lebel or swapping rum for flights along the Rivière Caniapiscau, I became lost, scared, and completely blown off course.

I tried to find comfort in history books, captains' logs, letters of sailors and prospectors, the elegies of missionaries and their converted heathens. But they only added to my knowledge of the peninsula's long and colourful history of devouring those who came with a purpose or quest, religious or commercial. I knew I had to go forward, but I didn't know which way; often a straight line became the longest route between two points, and the present could not be separated from the past. To survive, I learned that the difference between a step and a misstep lay in the ability to decipher the connections and collisions between the tightly ordered sequence of European conquest and the elliptical span of aboriginal resistance.

AT THE

EDGE

OF ALL

THINGS

I

CANIAPISCAU

1

As daylight broke on February 5, 1992, Martin wanted to surprise Catherine with a breakfast of eggs and caribou sausage, toast and coffee. On their first morning, he figured, they'd eat well and stick to the basics — water, firewood, and a few quick trips on the snowmobile to see if the animals were running. After months of bundling merchandise, and two hectic weeks of deliveries and drop-offs, pickups and exchanges, Martin wanted to thank her for her patience and her ability to adjust, despite last-minute changes and fly-by-night arrangements.

He wiggled out of his sleeping bag and stepped into his down-lined, Gore-Tex leggings. Flushed with the success of their journey out of Montreal, he was surprised by his desire to please. As he laced his boots and buttoned his shirt, he considered frying an onion and thawing out the jam as well, but told himself to back off. There would be other opportunities. He wrapped himself in his fluorescent green parka and rabbit-fur hat. Pulling on his gloves, he grabbed the plastic five-gallon bucket, then opened the plywood door and stepped outside.

He unhinged the axe from the side of the Bombardier and walked down the trail of packed snow left by the machine. At a thicket of stunted spruce and alder, he waded into the drifts beyond the riverbank. When his strides created a light crunch, as if he were stepping on brittle twigs, he knew it was safe to clear a spot and swing — the ice would be two metres thick.

Careful not to lose his balance or take a misstep into the elliptical hole made by his axe, he narrowed his world to the methodical swings. The movement stretched his muscles and pushed blood through his limbs. When a frozen chunk resisted his attack, he swung faster and harder until it broke. Then he stopped momentarily, repositioning the grip of his gloved hands on the varnished hickory handle, securing the placement of his feet. After his fourth or fifth burst of extra effort, he had to pause for a breather, and it was then he felt an odd sensation that something wasn't right. He listened intently for a moment, but heard nothing. Breath restored, he swung again, and the metal blade pierced the ice, sending chips into the air.

After a few swings, the tightening of his arm muscles forced him to wait again. That was when he heard the sound of two engines and picked up the smell of smoke.

Following the track he'd made coming down, he pushed through the drifts and climbed the short, steep incline between a brown-grey boulder and a black-and-beige-striped granite ledge.

The cabin was on fire. By the time he reached it, Catherine was already tossing snow and ice on the flames with the folding spade. Martin dropped his axe near the Bombardier, took the bucket, and furiously worked to contain the fire to one wall. Both of them could smell the kerosene that had been poured on the plywood sheets.

"We're never going to stop it," she said, watching the flames shoot into the corners. "There's no way."

He hustled a few more buckets of snow, but the fire was licking the second wall now, heading for a third. "You're right."

Catherine did not detect any panic as he dropped the bucket and grabbed the axe. "I can see the table and shelves," she told him, peering through the window. "The roof and crossbeams are still holding."

She pointed to a spot where the siding had become a charred veneer, and Martin positioned himself. Swinging again and again, he splintered the panels, opening a gash in the burning wall.

Catherine darted in for the sleeping bags and an armful of canned food; he grabbed the boxes of ammunition. They made a few more trips, picking up flashlights, maps, knapsacks, and the lantern. When he heard the loud tear above his head, Martin made one last dash, scooping three bottles of liquor and a case of cigarettes.

After the rafters fell, he used the spade to etch a path through the cinders. He stood in the middle of what had been the storage area and knew that their stash would raise suspicion amongst scavengers or police. Raising the spade over his head, he focused on the glass and metal that glistened in the morning sun. Then he wildly hacked at the remaining bottles of liquor and cans of food.

"Making it look like a robbery," he explained. "Okay. Let's take a long ride to confuse the cops."

They returned to the Rivière Caniapiscau, heading west from the triangular ridge that marked the Gorge des Bas. Though Martin Rouleau knew the wide channel was a thoroughfare for hunters crisscrossing the peninsula, he figured that loops and circles off the watercourse would serve his purpose. For a few minutes, they considered a run for the Hydro-Québec settlements, but agreed on the need to move erratically. As Martin drove, Catherine Boulanger wondered about her fear. Logic told her that Martin was right — attackers had hit them and run — but, she worried, how far? At each bend, she expected an ambush; each track seemed sinister. She wanted to scream.

Seeing the smoke swirl overhead, Martin figured the Hydro-Québec technicians would make the call. Hunters would veer off the path to pass the cabin out of curiosity and the desire to help, but rock doctors and engineers would notify the cops and send a chopper. With radios and their cellular emergency network, they could contact nearby switching stations or the company settlements at Brisay, Fontanges, Laforge. Given the gorge's hydrological importance and the scattering of cabins to the east, they would act quickly, Martin knew, investigating any possible threat to dams and dikes. Someone would be sent within a couple of hours.

As they pulled off the Caniapiscau and wound their way up a gentle incline that swerved behind the first level of sandstone terraces, Martin and Catherine spotted a group of travellers going northeast. He weighed the possibility of being recognized against their need for information and decided to risk a meeting. Catherine reluctantly agreed, hoping to discourage Martin from starting a chase. As the three snowmobiles took the bend to their left, Martin and Catherine emerged from the woods and flagged down the party: two Cree and one Québécois. Two of their sleds were filled with supplies, and on the back of the third were four animal carcasses. Caribou. No wolves. No marten, no beaver skins. The hunters had heard the animals were running to the north, and they hoped to make the old Fort McKenzie site by dark. When Martin asked them if they'd seen anyone earlier in the morning, each man shook his head.

"No one came from this direction," the Québécois said.

Throughout the morning, Martin and Catherine got the same answer from several groups heading north to the tree line and tight watersheds, where the caribou herd broke up and small clusters sought food and shelter.

Shortly before noon, they saw the police chopper. It went straight for the gorge, dipped over the ridge, and followed the spruce groves to the cabin's smouldering remains. Cutting away from the river, Martin and Catherine changed directions and picked up the tributaries that angled south between the slopes and bogs. To make sure that the cops would not detect their trail, they looped east, then took a sharp westerly turn to high ground, crested at a line of blue-green-and-grey rock. From there, Martin spotted four young men on two snowmobiles, with supplies on one sled and animals on the other. He eagerly approached.

They'd come the long way from Manicouagan to Lac Naskaupi, they said, then through Nitchequon and up the Caniapiscau. Hoping to prolong their journey, they were bartering for pelts to sell down south and hunting for meat. For most of the day tracks and hunches had taken them into the bush. Had they come across another party, said the oldest, who couldn't have been much more than twenty, then they were not doing their job.

When one of the group suggested a trade, Martin and Catherine declined but kept the conversation going, hoping to glean more information. Unfortunately there was little of value.

About a half hour after the helicopter left, they came across Cree hunters zipping in and out of the stunted alder that surrounded the bogs — eight men on six machines. Besides gas and food, tent and equipment, they carried eight full-sized caribou and two racks. They slowed at Martin's signal and motored to a meeting point between an incline of trees and a slab of granite. As the sun dimmed over the western rocks, the Cree quickly turned from greetings to questions.

"Did you see the police?" the elder asked.

"Overhead," Martin answered.

"We were just northeast of the gorge," the elder continued. "They asked us about a fire near the mouth of the Rivière du Sable."

Another hunter said, "They wanted to know if we'd seen the smoke. How about you?"

"A fire?" Catherine stayed completely still.

The elder nodded. "The inspector said a cabin had burned and people were inside but then got away. We were worried — perhaps they were some of our people from Nitchequon or stragglers who lived along the dams. Maybe from Mistassini or Lac St-Jean. But they were looking for somebody."

"What do you mean?"

"The inspector said he saw snowmobile tracks coming from the southwest and going into the Eaton Canyon." The elder turned to one of the men riding solo. "He even went up to my nephew here and asked if he wanted to give a statement."

"About the cabin," the younger man chimed in. "You're from here. You know which one, right?"

"Yes." Martin looked at Catherine, who gave a slight nod.

"When I told him I didn't know anything, he asked my uncle about the animals and the terrain."

Once again the elder spoke. "He wanted to know about the caribou. Seemed to think we'd stolen it from the burnt cabin. So I explained to him how the game starts to run on the far side, past the Eaton Canyon, up towards Lac Cambrien and even farther.

"The inspector shook his head. He didn't understand or he didn't want to listen. He thought I was telling him we caught the big herd running in this direction. He knew that only happened once in a while.

"You're right, I told him. The big runs don't happen here. In this area, we just get bunches of seven or eight, maybe a dozen. You have to pick off each animal.

"He looked right into my face and didn't say a word. I wondered what was going on, but it didn't matter that he suspected me. I told him the truth."

"You did the right thing." Martin worked hard to project empathy. "Did they ask anything else?"

"No, but I wouldn't have told him anyway." The elder smiled. "In the morning we came on two men without sleds."

"Heading into the Eaton Canyon," added the nephew. "They didn't have any equipment or supplies, just gas cans."

"But they stopped for us," said the elder. "It was strange. They warned us about the Gorge des Bas. From the beginning of the rapids, they said, near the first ridge, we'd see thick, black smoke rising into the sky. We moved off the watercourse and never got there in time. But they said it could be seen for six or seven kilometres."

With sunlight sliding into dull orange streaks, Martin and Catherine had yet to find a campsite, and Martin considered a spot near the burnt cabin. He pointed to the thin coils of grey-and-black smoke curling over the ridge. "It'd be safe to go there now," he told Catherine.

"Won't feel right," she replied. "Let's leave it. Find someplace else."

"That could be dangerous," he warned, then admitted his fear. "I don't know who to be afraid of, the police or our attackers."

She forced a laugh. "The cops don't give a shit about us. They saw the booze and cigarettes."

"Okay, but whoever burned us out is still looking for us."

"Maybe." She let her voice fall.

They took one more ride up the ridge to where the cabin had stood. Split beams and shingles still sizzled. The northwesterly wind carried the sharp odour of burnt wood and asphalt, kerosene and alcohol, melted plastic and consumed cardboard.

"You were right," he said. "We shouldn't stay here. Let's get what we can and go."

They tossed a few buckets of snow on the singed oil-drum stove and sections of galvanized pipe. After the hissing stopped, Martin worked on each joint with his chrome-plated wrenches. Together they rolled the drum to the sled.

Heading southeast, they slowly slalomed down two hills, then rode a stream that peeled off the gorge. Martin steered into an outcrop of beige-and-yellow-streaked granite. On the far side of these rocks, where a patch of snow and ice slanted down to a crooked line of trees, they found a spot.

"No one can see us from the main travel routes," he said. "It's perfect."

2

The wind changed direction and Martin woke up. By the glow of a lantern, he scanned the three spruce poles that supported the birch trunk running down the middle of the tent. As the canvas heaved with each gust, he thought about dressing and using the predawn hours to survey camp, inventory supplies, and scout routes for travel. But the flapping of the heavy cloth had him eyeing the knots that lashed the framing beams.

Before he could make a decision about what to do, he felt a burst of cold air. To the right of the tent opening, the canvas appeared to have split, allowing the chill to sweep into the three-by-four-metre shelter, shaking the poles and posts. He fidgeted with the lantern. The brass-plated control knob had frozen and he couldn't turn it to get the wick to give a stronger light.

Martin crept within reach of the oil-drum stove — there wasn't room to stand — placed the blade of his knife in the fire, and waited for the metal to glow. When his fingers could no longer stand the heat he tapped the hot blade against the chilled knob.

The noise awakened Catherine, who'd rolled onto her side and had a full view of the tent's front wall. There was a blast of wind, and the canvas flew open.

"Martin!" she gasped, pointing to a crossbeam that had slipped out of line.

He put down the knife and positioned himself at the left corner, tugging on the rope and pulling the canvas back into a firm wall. A moment later, the wind rattled the other corner.

"The whole fucking thing is falling apart," he barked.

Catherine scrambled to reinforce the other corner. As the rope blew free, Martin used his right hand to gather the loose ends, while his left caught the canvas. In a series of jerks and heaves, he positioned the spruce, then tossed the twine into crisscrossing ovals around the long, slender logs. Fighting the cold that numbed his fingers, he worked to thread his line and secure the knots. Again and again he tried, watching the twine weave in and out, then slip.

"I can't get the damn things to tighten," he said, grimacing.

"Can't help you," Catherine replied. Adjusting the posts and beams on her side took everything she had. She slid them left and jiggled, letting them roll into each other and straighten.

Martin twisted his torso and arms, then let go of the rope and allowed it to swing. The canvas fluttered, but the birch held, shifting only a few centimetres to the right. He checked the supports; they held once again and he grabbed the twine.

"It worked!" he shouted in surprise. "I don't know why, but it worked." He pulled so hard to make one last knot that the canvas tautened with a snap. For a moment everything shook.

"You scared me," Catherine said. "If you'd've messed up again, man, I'd really get pissed."

Confident now, he waved her off and moved deeper into the corner, making sure his knot was bound and the spruce secured. Then he used his forearm like a club to strike each piece of wood.

Nothing moved. The wind came and the canvas remained taut.

M artin needed to be alone. After bundling himself into his parka and hat, gloves and boots, he stepped outside. The first glimmers of daylight revealed a bulge beneath the hills that opened to the gorge, and he set off for it on his snowshoes. Remembering his grandfather's admonitions to shorten the stride when scaling a steep grade, he positioned himself on a blue-veined limestone terrace overlooking the Caniapiscau. He'd always wanted to hunt in this area, but he would not do so until the dams and reservoirs under construction were complete, reversing rivers and upending lakes. In his grandfather's time, the men saw the Labrador peninsula as one unbroken expanse of land, not a grid of transmission wires and canals, floodgates and dikes. What Martin saw was a landscape that was cut open, divided against itself, and stitched into odd shapes; his elders had spoken of an integrated territory stretching from the Rivière Saguenay, known to the Algonkians as the river of death, to the Monts Torngat, known to the Inuit as the home of evil spirits. For thousands of years, the various nations had kept themselves separate: the Attikamek were confined to the banks of the Saguenay and Lac St-Jean; the Cree hovered around Mistassini, extending their hunting grounds to the Monts Otish and Lac Nichicun; east of the Caniapiscau, between the Ashuanipi and the Rivière George, were the Naskapis, who called themselves the *nennenot* and moved through the woods and barrens; along the Côte du Nord roamed bands of hunters, whom the French lumped together as the Montagnais; the men and women the French dubbed Esquimaux, from the Algonkian description "eaters of raw flesh," dwelt on the far coast, where the rocks dropped directly into the sea.

Two generations before, when Martin's grandfather, a Naskapi, had come with his hunting party to the gorge searching for mountain lions in the cylindrical caves, the sharp cliffs and six-pointed crags alerted them that they had strayed into hostile territory. Outside their own land, they never set a base camp but kept moving from one stopping place to the next. After a fortnight, they returned east to the basin known as Michikamau.

Once a border, the gorge became an intersection. As Martin grew up, he saw the same physical conditions turn on a different geopolitical axis. In their efforts to lay claim to the land and exploit its minerals, white governments cast and recast names from their history: Labrador or Nouveau Québec, Nouvelle France or Canada, Newfoundland or Terre-Neuve. In their efforts to resist these divide-and-conquer strategies, the original inhabitants gave the land their own names — Utshimassit or Sheshashit for the Innu, Kawawachikamach for the Naskapi, Pakuashipi or Ushuat at Maliotenam for the Montagnais. As a teenager and young adult, Martin had watched them fight and lock themselves into bitter competition over the meaning of borders that had come into existence only within the last few hundred years. To Martin, their lines were invisible; it was one peninsula of many nations.

His grandfather was right. The land was an unbroken expanse of forest and barrens.

But Martin had learned the hard way. He'd witnessed, while a student at the Schefferville school, the creation of settlements and mines that turned his world upside down. He remembered the priests stepping up to the map and explaining how the government of Quebec joined with Hydro-Québec to create nine Montagnais settlements, each with its own band council, protected territory, and government budget. Martin's mother had wanted to move to the reserve outside Sept-Îles, but his father had refused, determined to hold on to his construction job with the mining and power companies. That, he told her, was the only future.

By the time Martin qualified for college, he saw that these new communities had little to offer young men, despite the heated debates over sovereignty and self-determination. While the Montagnais had formed alliances with the Attikameks, the unity promises of band-council politicians quickly turned into a new set of maps and borders that drew lines around hunting territories.

"White people are now giving us the chance to pick ourselves apart," he told his father. The older man could not disagree.

At university, Martin hated his classes, but learned to love books and the library. He read about the slick manoeuvres that allowed the newly formed Council of Attikameks and Montagnais to gain provincial recognition in Quebec while ignoring their cousins who lived across the invisible line in Newfoundland. There, more than 1500 people were crammed into the communities of Sheshashit near North-West River and Utshimassit at Davis Inlet. The rhetoric of solidarity and up-risings moved in and out of the newspapers, and Martin read the writings of geologists and anthropologists, archaeologists and cultural historians, learning that his home was a billion-year-old configuration of rocks that still pushed and pulled with the tides of the Atlantic, the Gulf of St. Lawrence, the Bay of Ungava. The peninsula was formed by volcanic eruptions, which tossed mountains upside down and turned seas inside out; the waves of heat and thrust were repeatedly chilled by winds and sheets of ice. As the glaciers retreated, they cut into the rocks, scooping out rivers and lakes.

Martin looked at slivers of daylight entering the gorge. He wanted to believe that it was still one peninsula, *his* peninsula.

The watercourses and ridges might still be locked into the ancient patterns of erosion, but he knew that machines could compress into a week what in prehistory had been an epoch. An esker created over millions of years could now be blown apart and demolished within hours. As the clock and calendar replaced the old standards of season, distances had shrunk: the 550,000 square kilometres of the peninsula could be tra-versed in six hours. Martin could take off from Tadoussac at dawn and be in Goose Bay by sundown; the hunt was choreographed to the drone of a snowmobile covering 200 kilometres a day.

He knew his attackers were no doubt far away now, but he still couldn't figure out what they'd been after. With the success of his deliveries — secrets being hard to keep in small, isolated communities — word must have got out. As he'd made his rounds in the late spring and summer of 1991, he knew he was working on the biggest deal of his life; the front money paid for a cabin in the middle of the peninsula, where all travel options remained. He hadn't broadcast the location, but he had used an airplane to deliver building supplies and food, a move that telegraphed activity. When the weather changed and early September offered its usual tranquillity, he took ten days to complete construction in full view of any traveller.

The cabin was more than a dream or a refuge; it was his place in his land. After leaving Schefferville in the 1970s and building his business over two decades, he believed that his success earned him a peaceful return. His triumph would be in the quiet comfort of the two- or three-month-long hunt, in having the time and equipment to journey from one end of the peninsula to the other. Catherine's unexpected friendship only added to the enjoyment. And now the cabin was burnt to the ground.

They didn't steal a thing, he told himself. They just destroyed his vision.

He'd always seen one peninsula, but now he was unsure. Staring into the gorge, he realized that the fire had consumed his connection to his homeland. While his grandfather's tales and his father's labours were supposed to fix his location, Martin knew that their experiences had lost their immediate hold on him. If he wanted to recapture their voices, he had to risk a journey into their past and solve the present mystery of who was stalking him.

He could not rely on his business, nor his knowledge of facts and dates, names and places. To survive he had to work day by day, hour by hour. As he headed back to the tent, he wondered if he had the discipline of his ancestors.

The burnt-orange streaks of dawn skimmed down the iced slopes and bounced off the green-grey crags. Catherine stood beside the uncovered sled and stretched. With her body fully extended, the top of her head exceeded his.

"You're making plans," Martin teased, noticing the grimace on her narrow face.

"Look at the food," she shot back. "What do we have? Less than ten days' worth?"

He glanced at the containers, filled to less than a quarter of their capacity. "Maybe two."

"Don't mess around." Her full lips drew down in a scowl. "I'm serious."

"Okay. Probably eight."

They'd left Montreal and started their trip with a full sled, at least six weeks' worth of food in boxes and cans, bottles and jars, most unloaded at the cabin and arranged in neat stacks. With the cabin as their base, they'd planned trips onto the barrens towards Ungava and beyond.

"We need to regroup," she said. "I don't know if we can do this."

"And good morning to you." He looked for the amber glitter in her black eyes that signified amusement, but couldn't find it.

"I'm not laughing." Catherine kept her voice in its slow, deliberate alto. "On our first morning someone tried to kill us. On our second the winds almost blew us away."

"You're scared," Martin said.

Catherine hesitated. "Yes."

"I know." He widened his long, triangular face into a smile. "This trip is far too dangerous."

"What about Schefferville?" She saw his body incline towards her, his chocolate-brown eyes asking for an embrace. "We can try my relatives."

"No good." Martin pulled back and shook his head, wisps of long back hair mixed with grey escaping from beneath the fur-lined ear flaps of his cap. "Word would get around. We need to stay out of sight until we can figure out who's chasing us and why."

Relieved that he'd retreated but angered at his response to her suggestion, she mocked him. "So you want to stay here."

"Of course not." He allowed himself a small laugh. "But I'm too scared to go anyplace else." He turned and walked into the tent, then out again, fortifying a pole, tugging on a knot. "It'll hold while we try to make sense of this."

"You really want to stay here?"

"I don't see any choice." He picked up a long stick and knocked it against the stovepipe and metal fastenings, listening for the rattle of a loose joint. Nothing.

"Day to day?"

"At some point, we'll have to head for a settlement." He stooped to make a snowball and throw it at the tent's front wall, then made two more to hurl at the sides. Each hit made a muffled thud on the canvas. "Whether we get to Schefferville or Kujjuaq, even slip over the Monts Otish towards Baie-Comeau, I don't know."

"It's scary."

"Yeah." He returned to the sled, where he pulled out his chain saw and five-gallon gas canister. "They want us to be afraid. They want us to make a mistake."

"Like staying out here."

"Look, I don't want to argue." He'd let his anger show, then turned away, embarrassed. He bent down to adjust the webbing and straps of his snowshoes and, still avoiding her gaze, picked up the chain saw and gas canister. He headed off, following the snowmobile track for several hundred metres to the edge of the grove, then climbed a small mound overlooking a stream. As the slope eased down towards the stream, Martin found what he needed — tall, straight, barren juniper, dried out by winter. Catherine heard the saw rip and put on her snowshoes to go after him.

When she spotted him, he appeared to be legless, the drifts covering his short, thick thighs. She wanted to laugh at the

17

sight of a broad-shouldered, barrel-chested torso moving over the snow, but she remained angry about his decision. When the third trunk fell beside the other two, she yelled over the growl of the saw, "I'm trying to save your stubborn ass, and you want to stay here forever!" He gave no indication of hearing.

After toppling the fourth tree, he switched off the saw and watched Catherine approach. Her long-legged stride down the path he'd created was nearly double his. Once in hearing distance, she tried again. "Don't expect me to move this fuckin' timber. It's all yours."

He switched on the saw again and trimmed the branches, hoping to call her bluff. When it came time to roll the trunks and drag them into position for the snowmobile, she remained silent and still.

"Come on," he said, hunching over.

Catherine kept silent. She knew an offer was forthcoming.

"I'll stay and do this," he proposed. "You go back, get the machine and some rope."

"You walk," she countered, "and I drive."

"You sit on the seat, while I tie them up and sweat," he shot back, grabbing one of the trunks.

"That's right."

"Sounds like a deal," he chuckled. "I'll size them for the stove."

An hour and a half later, after two of the junipers were cut into logs and placed beside the tent, Martin stashed his saw on the sled and pulled out the insulated polypropylene boxes containing their fresh food. He took four links of caribou sausage and then removed six eggs. With a frozen loaf of bread, an onion, a frosted stick of butter, and a jar of marmalade, he was ready for breakfast. He threw snow into the percolator and went into the tent.

"At least you know enough to cook for me," Catherine teased. "After being dragged all this way, I deserve one good meal."

3

Madeleine Rouson summoned what was left of her strength to climb the stairs to Martin's Montreal apartment. The spacious four-room flat off the rue Ottawa was on the third floor of what used to be a warehouse for machine parts, tool cutters, grinders, and die casters. It had been vacated in the late 1960s, then claimed by squatters and students during the FLQ crisis. According to the romantic exaggerations of neighbourhood lore, the building had become a bomb factory and hideout. The redbrick structure was abandoned during the final days of the struggle and fell into disrepair until the real-estate boom of the early 1970s. Then it was purchased by a syndicate of downtown lawyers and bankers, and renovated into fifteen apartments in the hope of attracting upscale tenants. Martin moved in during the recession of the late 1980s.

When she'd agreed to live there, Madeleine knew that Martin stayed in Montreal from May until January, working the city for cash to buy his supplies and outfit needed for the winter hunt. Though he told her this would be his first year in the cabin, Madeleine knew he might go anywhere — Caniapiscau, Natashquan, Battle Harbour. He'd talked of his travels past Nain, up into the Kiglapaits or Torngats, then down the back side to Ungava.

He didn't seem to recall it, but Madeleine was sure their first meeting had been ten years earlier. She'd been lining up for the train from Sept-Îles to Schefferville, and he'd been loading his snowmobile and supplies for a hunt. While she was going north to visit her parents for Mardi Gras Montagnais, he planned to meet some old friends and head for the Rivière George.

During the ten-hour train ride they talked, casting themselves as two of the "renegades" who made it off the peninsula by completing school and wandering through a couple of years of university. They shared a few laughs about the differences in the mission schools at Schefferville and Sept-Îles, where she'd graduated. After Madeleine had made it to Laval and the Université de Montréal, her father was one of those who moved back to Schefferville, where he'd found a job through the provincial government. When she'd started to flunk out, the old man had tried to get her back, but the allure of city streets and fast money had taken hold.

When Martin gave her a wink of encouragement, she felt comfortable and gave him the rundown on a life that had turned into a string of misplaced encounters with employers, boyfriends, married men, dope dealers, cops, probation officers, and social workers. On the lam, she tried working her way back to the peninsula and hiding in Schefferville. She never made it.

"I like cocaine," she admitted. "Always have."

He touched her hand. "Don't worry."

Nothing happened between them other than pleasant conversation. A few days after their arrival at Schefferville, she heard of his departure for the bush. Madeleine's tastes led her back to the city and a few extended stays in Baltimore and

Philadelphia, Manhattan and Boston, as cocktail waitress and dancer, petty thief and jailbird. She figured that thirty days of guaranteed shelter and food was better than bouncing around in buses and sleeping in rooms at the YWCA.

Throughout her odd journey, Madeleine kept in touch with Catherine Boulanger, a school buddy who had similar habits but had never fallen as far. Madeleine jumped on the train to Montreal when a dope deal turned sour in New York.

By that time, Catherine had hooked up with Martin. He'd pieced together a deal that was to be the biggest score of his life and offered Madeleine a place to stay if she agreed to help.

Martin had met Catherine on a sweltering, starless July night in 1990, one week into the showdown that became the Oka crisis. Frequently travelling the St. Lawrence, he'd become a member of the so-called Mohawk Navy, a loosely organized group of men who ferried guns, ammunition, food and money to the protesters. Though one or two of these skippers were Iroquois, the Mohawks called on trusted outsiders, because they did not want to have one of their own caught on the river with guns and bullets. Martin knew they couldn't trust a white boy to do this, so he'd answered the underground call for Indian volunteers and immediately proved acceptable; the Mohawks knew he'd been working with buttleggers for years.

During the eighty days of escalating confrontations at Oka and the Mercier Bridge, Martin had faithfully responded to radio calls, smuggling contraband and shuttling Mohawk Warriors in and out of the battle zone. From the marsh around the point at St-Anicet in southwestern Quebec, he'd race his fourteen-footer up the St. Lawrence. Once he'd pulled into shore, he would straddle the boat, one rubber boot sinking into the slop, the other perched on the aluminium gunwale, while he stacked radio sets and boxes of canned food, and tobacco in the hull. He'd keep his hunting rifle in the open and stuff a couple of AK-47s into separate olive-drab U.S. Army duffel bags amongst the fishing and hunting gear in the bow. Then he'd push off and zoom back to the Île Perrot, where he'd cut the motor and putt-putt into Lac des Deux Montagnes. Steering between the red-lighted buoys that marked the channels, he'd look for green lights on the shore, which would direct him to a drop manned by the Mohawks who'd built the barricades.

It was on one of these trips that he spotted Catherine. She stood above the others, a distinct olive hue to her pale brown skin, hair unbraided. She was a Montagnais, and one of the Indians who'd come from all over Canada to help the Mohawks. She recognized him as a Naskapi; he had the typical compacted limbs and long, broad torso, the reddish ochre tinge to his walnut skin.

She insisted they'd met in Schefferville or Sept-Îles, or at least somewhere on the Côte du Nord. After so many years of travelling back and forth, Martin couldn't remember.

"At least we have something in common," she told him. "We started in the same place."

Before the Canadian Armed Forces closed in on Oka, Catherine introduced him to Madeleine. They continued to assist the Mohawks, but Martin worried that the women would be caught in the crossfire as the soldiers successfully began to set one faction against another and take control. He provided them with an escape that eventually took them to Toronto.

The two women returned to Montreal the next year, in early July of 1991. Broke and strung out, they wanted to get back to the peninsula. They asked Martin for a few days of shelter and food, maybe two or three quick dope runs to score enough money for plane tickets. Martin arranged a couple of small transactions, but Catherine and Madeleine used the proceeds to steal and sell credit cards, cash, jewellery, and tobacco, while he went north to build the cabin. When he returned, their success surprised him; they were running a streak that had brought each of them more than $1500 a week.

In exchange for their labour, he offered a wage from his transport business, which involved tobacco runs, dope deals, and dabbling in liquor and tools, fuel oil and building supplies. He needed someone to watch the apartment, keep track of messages, make the occasional cash drop or pickup. After they tended to his business, Catherine and Madeleine would be free, he said, to take care of their own.

They agreed.

Catherine concentrated on the details. She understood Martin's need to work quietly and efficiently, keeping in the shadows of the Corsicans, Mohawks, Québécois, Sicilians, Americans, Haitians, Nigerians, Moroccans, Lebanese, Greeks, and Italians. She wanted the business to succeed — security first, cash and a good time later — and played the percentages; she knew that crime had got her into this mess and crime could get her out.

Madeleine stuck to the long shot; she bought new clothes and, working the rue Ste-Catherine after midnight, partied and shimmied with boys and girls eager for eightballs and bumpers, thrills that gave her easy cash.

For a while she considered it cookie-jar money: a C-note here, two bills there, a quick taste and a long night that always broke into an uneventful dawn. She tried to be careful, choosing marks from the middle classes, the respectable bourgeoisie who always had to get up in the morning and dress for the office or to open the store. They were young, with careers and nice apartments, or middle-aged, with cars and credit cards. A few were lesbians; some were bisexuals with a yen for triangles. But most were straight guys who loved the combination of cocaine and a dark-skinned woman.

By mid-November her expenses began to equal her earnings, and this presented Martin with a dilemma: kick her out, risk her arrest, and the possibility of the police turning her into a snitch, or keep her in the apartment, risk mistakes, and the possibility of exposure to rivals. As he and Catherine prepared to go north, he wracked his brain for a solution. Madeleine was not fit for the rigours of a journey into the bush, nor was she capable of working in someone else's organization. Her charm, intelligence, and wit were at once her greatest strengths and her greatest weaknesses. She was a loner, yet could not survive without a helping hand.

Martin struggled to an acceptable compromise: if Madeleine kept the apartment clean and avoided trouble until the second week of February, she'd be sent a plane ticket for passage to

Sept-Îles; he'd arrange for $2000 in cash to be waiting. As he told her, "The incentive is yours."

Madeleine worked hard to control her late-night escapades, limiting her fun to a few dreamers and voyeurs. She recognized the chance that Martin and Catherine were giving her and pulled back from the short cons and quick thefts. If nothing else, she told herself, she owed it to her friends to accept the opportunity. Going back to the peninsula was much better than going back to jail or going out to the rue Ste-Catherine. So she kept a low profile, preparing for her return.

On the morning of February 6, 1992, she came back to the apartment feeling good after completing her part of a dope deal that brought her $500.

The door had been kicked in.

After breakfast, Martin sat in contemplative silence by the stove. He locked his fingers around his enamel-and-metal mug, hoping the heat would seep through his skin and into his muscles. The coffee, dark and bitter with chicory and cinnamon, pleased him. He always prepared several kilos in Montreal, then stashed it in ordinary grocery cans, which he packed separately from the containers of food. He accepted his dependence on several nonessentials: coffee, toilet paper, toothpaste. Face it, he told himself. You've lived most of your life in the city.

And that was what worried him this morning. The attack demonstrated that he'd become an outsider. On what he thought of as his own turf, he could no longer, it seemed, command the respect or authority that went unchallenged. Now he had to respond.

His mind wanted to race through schemes, but he focused on sketching the scene and establishing certainties; standing on the river, he'd heard the snowmobiles coming from the southwest; at the burning cabin, he'd smelled kerosene; there'd been no attempt to steal.

The operation had been simple. The attackers came, doused the wall, ignited it, and took off to the northeast. The facts were clear, the intent mysterious. Was the blaze a warning? A punishment? An attempt to kill? Of course it could have been the demented prank of teens or young men strung out on glue or gas, dope or booze. But he didn't think so. He was certain this attack was executed, on contract, for a purpose. Someone wanted to hurt him. From Montreal to Nain, Sept-Îles to Kujjuaq, he'd run contraband and supplies for more than fifteen years, working the peninsula as a hunter, dealer, trader, smuggler. There were dozens of men who might be angry or feel cheated by fast appearances and fast deals for fast dollars. Now, after he'd pulled off the biggest deal of his life, someone wanted to slow him down.

Was it a warning?

Arson gave its victims a chance to get away. It terrified and destroyed without wounding. If the attackers had started in the southwest, they'd followed his track and spotted his parked snowmobile. Seeing smoke coming out of the pipe, they'd had to figure the cabin was occupied. Their work would at least have forced Martin out into the cold without equipment and supplies.

They wanted him naked and alone. Desperate.

That would lead to the worst kind of death. Freezing, stiffening, lungs contracting. He saw himself without a parka, without gloves, without boots, riding a snowmobile and dragging the sled in a pathetic and futile search for help.

This conclusion shook him onto another line of thought. His attackers deliberately ignored the oil and fuel, food and tools, apparently content simply to torch his cabin. If they wanted Martin to die, they could have messed with the snowmobile. They could have slashed his snowshoes, stolen his weapons from the sled.

So they didn't want to kill.

Looking at Catherine on the other side of the stove, he wondered if her presence had altered their plans. She said she hadn't heard their approach and only woke up to the crackling of flames; Martin considered the possibility that their assailants had spotted her inside. As they'd rounded the cabin, pouring kerosene, they'd had the opportunity to peer through the window and see the sleeping bag positioned by the stove.

They had the chance to shoot, he thought, a quick pop. But they didn't.

"You're turning it over and over in your mind, aren't you?" Catherine asked, pouring coffee into her white porcelain mug.

He needed a moment to answer truthfully. "I'm thinking about you."

She didn't respond.

Uncomfortable with her silence, he started again. "Did they see you and run?"

"Does it matter?"

Martin shrugged. "I want to know why it happened this way. They could've killed you or just destroyed our supplies."

"You're going to drive yourself crazy," she said between sips of coffee.

"I'm looking for clues." He reached over and refilled his cup. "There has to be a reason for this."

She smiled. "So now you're an investigator?"

"No." He chuckled. "I'm a hunter."

She chuckled too. "And a crook."

After a long gulp, he returned to the subject. "There has to be something that gives them away."

"If you know why they attacked you," she reasoned, "then you might know who."

"That's right." His gaze sought hers. "And all I know is they could've killed us, but didn't. I think someone wanted us to live."

Catherine shook her head. "You're a hunter. You're looking for a hoofprint, a track, a scent. And you believe you'll find them. But it doesn't work like that. If someone is after you, then they have your track. They know how to get to you."

His body twisted away from her as if he were trying to dodge something. "I'm being hunted," he said.

"That's right." She finished her coffee and stepped outside.

S eventeen days earlier, on January 20, Catherine had rolled out of bed before the alarm and grabbed the fully packed black-and-green nylon knapsack that stood against the bedroom wall. Dragging it to the beige tweed couch in the living room, she checked and double-checked each compartment, mumbling, "Six pairs of socks, six shirts, four pairs of leggings, four bras, extra gloves, extra hat."

Slivers of sunlight slid onto the floor as she finished her task. She settled at the oval oak table, with a cup of instant coffee and two slices of dry toast, positioning her chair to face the window. Outside, the violet glow receded, giving way to a yellow-red-shaded clarity that outlined the angular grid of buildings and streets.

As she sat there, her fear of being misled or misunderstanding Martin's needs and his business dealings increased. He'd never before put together a deal that moved such a large amount of inventory, and she worried about being used as his dupe and floozy, a lackey and a piece of ass, who lured customers and carried messages. In her past, too many deals had come and gone; too many friends bought and bartered, sold and traded. If Martin was going to cut her loose, this would be the time.

She fully expected it. She expected to hear the alarm, hear him get out of bed, grunt and groan as he stretched, then deliver the news.

The alarm went off at six forty-five. She heard Martin gasp and fumble to shut off the buzzer. She took her dishes into the kitchen, washed them, and walked into the bedroom.

"You ready to travel?" he asked without looking up from making the bed.

"Yes," she answered, her calm response concealing her anxiety.

At Dorval, after they'd picked up the tickets purchased under false names, Catherine wondered if she should tell him about her attack of fear. As they stood in the gangway, waiting to board the flight to Quebec City, she only nodded and said nothing.

M artin directed the taxi through the Lower Town to make sure they weren't being followed. They curved through the antique district and turned west on the rue St-Pierre. Zigzagging behind the Musée de la Civilisation, the driver pulled up to a fashionable café less than a block from the Place Royale. They treated themselves to a full complement of coffee, juice, and pastries, taking their time and savouring the discomfort they'd created amongst customers dressed for the office. At noon they met their connection in front of l'Église Notre Dame des Victoires.

During the ride to Baie-Ste-Catherine, Martin asked the man about the arrangements and schedules. He replied that Beverly Papineau had assembled a crew in the weeks before Christmas, alerting them to the imminent possibility of work. By New Year's, she'd rounded up the fleet of two vans, two Toyota pickups, a Jeep Cherokee, a Honda Accord, three snowmobiles, and Martin's fourteen-foot boat. When the first load of cargo had arrived, it crossed the mouth of the Saguenay in darkness, six runs to the glazed shoals at Pointe-aux-Vaches. The cigarettes and whisky had been quickly stashed in the vans and driven to the warehouse near Anse-à-la-Cave.

At Baie-Ste-Catherine, Martin and Catherine boarded the same boat and sat huddled in the stern while the pilot navigated the Saguenay's tides and thin sheets of ice. Approaching the wharf at Tadoussac, the aluminium hull swung starboard to loop around the larger berths and find a slip beside the harbourmaster's shed. Martin and Catherine were immediately taken to the Honda and driven out of town.

Martin, pleased by the efficiency of the operation, remained silent as they veered off Route 138 and followed a dirt-and-gravel track to a granite ledge surrounded by tall pines. The prefabricated metal structure that sat on the ledge was invisible from the road and the water. As he and Catherine walked through the steel door, Beverly Papineau rose from her dented grey desk in one corner.

"Another day, another dollar," she said to Martin, while extending a hand to Catherine. "I'm always glad my credit's good."

Martin smiled at the joke, and Beverly led them to another corner, where cases of motor oil were stacked against the wall. "Let's not bother to settle up now," he said so that the crew members, who were also in the room, could hear. "If you had to pay it all, you'd go broke and too many people would lose their jobs."

"That's right." Beverly jabbed him in the shoulder. "It's always good to have a sugar daddy." She began to disperse the crowd.

As he and Catherine sat down on the boxes, Martin noticed the others darting wary glances at the newcomer. He let the content of his remarks speak for Catherine's reliability, launching into a discussion of prices and percentages, deliveries and schedules, regarding the shipment consolidated in Quebec City. "Once the money changes hands," he said, "the airplane can be loaded."

"Do you know where we stand?" Beverly asked.

"I'm up about $20,000," Martin answered. "But there's nothing to worry about."

"You really are moving big quantities." She paused to make sure the others were out of earshot. "No one expected this. No one has enough for it all."

Martin gave a dismissive wave. "I've been working too long to screw up this kind of score." He leaned forward. "Let's clean it up first and then we can talk about the national economy."

Acknowledging the wisecrack with a twitch of her lips, Beverly pulled a pen from the pocket of her jeans and began to scribble on one of the cases. Instead of paying Martin in advance as she was supposed to, she was running a tab that revolved around a base price of 45 to 55 cents a pack and six dollars a bottle. "You're still covering for me, right?"

"Depends how much you can take." He waited to see if she'd object. "I can carry up to $30,000, maybe $35,000, but the Corsicans are on my back. They're always edgy."

"Why?" Beverly was obviously trying to nudge him into divulging more details of his arrangement in Montreal. "You treat them right. They've never been shorted."

He shook his head. "You know better than to dig into other people's business. It's time to work our deal."

She returned to her calculations.

Martin started again. "As long as I come back and make good — " he paused " — then they don't have to know who I deal with. Understand?"

Beverly nodded. "That means I can't push you much further."

"I'm holding $20,000 of yours already, and there's a very big order coming." Martin glanced at Catherine, who remained perfectly still.

Beverly put her pen down and took a step beyond Catherine's left shoulder. She crossed to a pile of cardboard boxes marked PAPER TOWELS and PULP PRODUCTS. "This kind of volume makes it tight for you — " she met Martin's eyes " — doesn't it?"

"I have a lot of inventory to move." That was as direct an answer as he would give.

"I don't know what we can do," Beverly said, taking the top box and setting it before Martin. He cut the packing tape and pushed his hand through the layer of rolls wrapped in cellophane, yanking out a neatly bundled wad of $100 bills.

"You know I like round numbers," she told him.

He flicked her a smile. "You always have."

"But I can't take it all," she added. "You'll have to work with me, especially if you're worried about holding a debt."

He tried to push her. "I want to get rid of everything. Clean it all up here."

"There's too much, and besides, that means you'd have to wait for me to pay you," Beverly replied. "I don't want the pressure. Not this time. I just want to buy a share and let you have the rest."

He took a moment to fully comprehend her proposal. "You'll buy a fixed amount — one shot?" he asked. "I get the money and you get the goods, right?"

"Yeah. What's left over is yours. You can fly out of here, make the deliveries, and collect."

"But we're settled on this once you get your share?"

Beverly nodded. "That's right. Nice and simple."

"And I just hold the 20 grand?"

"No. You'll forgive it." She chuckled. "We've done business for a long time."

"Let's keep it that way." He stood and waved to one of Beverly's workers, gesturing for paper and a pen. "What's the number?"

"I've got $211,000 American," she said, pointing to the boxes marked PULP PRODUCTS. "And $11,200."

He stepped around Catherine and positioned himself beside the pile of boxes. Working the calculations, he offered a selling price of $5.25 per carton of cigarettes.

"Can I do a little bit better?" she asked. "At $5, we'll come out with even numbers."

"Trying to work me over, huh?"

Everyone grinned as Beverly stepped forward to look over his shoulder and tap his ass. "Just work the numbers."

"What do I get?"

She leaned on the boxes marked TOOLS and SCREWDRIVERS. "All the coastal drops."

Martin was impressed. He returned to his calculations and offered to sell 42,200 cartons for the $211,000 and 1800 bottles of booze for the $11,200. As for his remaining inventory of 40,000 cartons and 400 bottles, he planned to sell them at retail prices. "I could sell them to you for 200 grand," he told Beverly, "but if I keep the plane here and just hop up and down from Betsiamites to St-Augustin or Goose Bay, I'll double my money. Same with the booze."

"So, I'm giving you a chance to earn back the $20,000 and a lot more, right?"

"It's fair."

"Martin," she said, "it's better than fair."

"If everything goes right — " he watched his hand complete the arithmetic " — you'll make a little bit more than $200,000 net."

"And you could take in well over $400,000." Beverly allowed herself a smile. "Remember, I know the game."

"All right." Martin offered his hand. "We still need each other."

∾

On the morning of January 21, Antoine Danielle landed at the strip outside Grande des Begerrones. His single-engine Piper was carrying the first of sixteen loads for the territories up the Saguenay and along the Côte du Nord. Boxed and bundled as disposable diapers, canned food, dishwashing soap, and screwdrivers, the cargo was tossed into vans and trucks, driven to Beverly's shed, broken down, and picked up for distribution around Alma, Lac St-Jean, and beyond. The plane tried to make two deliveries in the morning and two in the afternoon; Beverly's crews worked late, one team assigned to unloading, another to warehousing, and a third to driving. Within hours after their arrival, cigarettes rolled towards Jonquière and Chicoutimi.

When Antoine told her he'd need another three days to complete her end of the load, Beverly just shrugged. "I've been doing this for years," she said. "You know that. We'll get through and bring back the money."

∾

The next afternoon brought a steady snowfall, and Antoine made his last run in darkness. But the winds died down, allowing the storm to hover for an extra twelve hours. That shut them down for a day. Despite the grounding, Beverly's drivers pushed on, reaching their destinations and rolling back for some unexpected hours of sleep. As the weather cleared after dinner, the plane took off and deliveries resumed. Meanwhile, Catherine joined Martin in locating customers for his portion of the shipments. Crammed into the shed, they used Beverly's phone. Martin made contact and Catherine juggled the numbers to arrange for two or three extra deliveries. Could they get 6000 cartons to Goose Bay by February 1? Sept-Îles could take 7000 for a new shopping centre. And Baie-Comeau, what about the people there? An extra 3500 cartons? Okay. A few thousand more? Sure.

After Antoine finished moving the merchandise, Martin laid out his plan, asking Catherine to accompany them for the drops up the coast. "One after another," he explained, "from southwest to northeast."

The next morning offered bits of sunshine between the squalls, and they flew to Pointe Lebel,where the runway overlooked the mouth of the Manicouagan River. Unloaded into a new truck operated by a group from the Betsiamites reserve, 5500 cartons fetched top price, and dealers set off for customers as far away as Pointe-aux-Anglais and Rivière Pentecôte. On January 27, they took off in clear skies, adding twelve free cases of liquor for Antoine's relatives at Ushuat at Maliotenam, the Indian territory hooked on the point that opens to the Moisie.

Antoine's mother had married a Québécois and moved into town, but she'd never forgotten her family on the reserve. Throughout his years at the Jesuit school, Antoine's cousins had been in and out of his life. At eighteen he'd enlisted in the Canadian Armed Forces, hoping to learn aviation skills and break out of the town's insular community. Instead of Europe, the command had posted him with NATO crews at Goose Bay.

"I joined the forces to see the world, but I never got past Labrador," he told Catherine, twisting his round, sienna face into a sly grin. "After twelve years of fixing choppers and planes, I wanted to be a pilot. So I left with enough money to buy my own plane."

He'd walked away from the military and started his own business, flying everywhere on the Côte du Nord and north into the bush — for Hydro-Québec, the mining companies, the geologists, the foresters, anybody who needed to go up.

He'd become a common sight on these routes and heard talk of Martin, who'd been making the rounds of settlements, radar stations, airstrips. "That's how we met," he said. It took another four days to make the drops at Mignan, Havre St-Pierre, Natashquan, St-Augustin, and Goose Bay. Dodging the winter storms, Antoine's Piper dipped in and out of the clouds that masked the forests. Catching the northwestern wind as it blew over the V-shaped harbour at Masquaro or circling around the Îles de Grande Passe at the entrance to Baie-St-Augustin, he flipped the rudder and jerked the throttle in short, choppy motions that sent the plane into a bump and grind. "The single-engine two-step," he joked, "a dance that rocks and rolls."

When the drops were finished, they'd collected another $415,000, giving them a total of $626,000, when added to the cash provided by Beverly. They returned to Tadoussac and gave themselves two days off, eating big meals at restaurants, shopping for gloves and flares, getting Martin's gun cleaned and oiled, paying for the Bombardier, buying canned goods and provisions, a new set of tools and ropes, compasses and maps. On the morning of February 2 Martin and Catherine counted out $25,000 Canadian for their trip, and Antoine took another $25,000. The remaining $576,000 was stuffed into three large, double-sealed boxes, while the $11,200 worth of greenbacks were kept in a knapsack. That afternoon they piled their money and gear into one of Beverly's trucks and drove to the airstrip.

They flew into the clouds over Chibougamau, where Martin and Catherine picked up the Bombardier. Then Antoine gave them their last ride, flying to Nitchequon, landing directly east of the lake and south of the settlement. On February 3 they drove the Bombardier to the Hydro-Québec site at Caniapiscau. They traded six cartons of cigarettes, two bottles of liquor, and $10 for a room in the village, and spent most of the night listening to the river running through the massive powerhouse and its groaning turbines. They headed out at dawn, arriving at the cabin as the bronze sun swung out of the southern sky and started its descent beyond the western edge of the Gorge des Bas.

The next morning was February 5.

"You think we were followed from the beginning," Catherine said, dipping her cup in the snow, then using her gloved fingers to wash it out.

"It's the only way I can make sense of what happened," Martin replied.

"You can trace it back all the way to Montreal." She paused. "Everyone knows you leave town at this time."

He nodded. "It's hardly a secret. It could've been anybody from anywhere."

"Might have nothing to do with cigarettes or liquor."

"I know." He stepped outside and grabbed a twenty-litre gas can from the sled. By the time he'd placed it on the Plexiglas platform moulded into the back of the snowmobile's chassis, Catherine had joined him. "Even if there isn't any real chance of finding anybody, I have to see if there's some trail. My mind keeps telling me to go out and look."

"Of course."

Shortly after 10:00 a.m., they began their run to the Eaton Canyon. They slipped over the ridges on the Caniapiscau's northern banks and sliced through groves of black spruce, eager to avoid the heavily travelled waterway. They curved into marshes and tributaries that offered the possibility of fowl or game, then moved on an eastward arc that crossed a frozen wetland. When a double line of caribou prints ran beside their path, Martin stopped for a quick examination. The impressions, crusted with ice and covered by a layer of blown snow, appeared to be at least six hours old. The animals must have run in darkness, the strongest wind at their backs.

Martin caught sight of three ptarmigans near a thicket of alder that angled down a 200-metre hill. A good shot required him to wheel the machine to the right, then dismount into two metres of snow. By then his prey would be long gone.

So they continued. Catherine settled on the back of the vinyl seat, Martin hunched on the front, his arms and shoulders easily steering the machine along the slope. As the early afternoon dipped over their shoulders, the harsh yellow-and-white fluorescence fused into a gilded light.

The canyon appeared after the last set of turns, two elbow-shaped paths between blue-green boulders and the scraggly spruce and larch. It opened to the Rivière Caniapiscau. Split by rocky brown islands that pierced the snow and ice, the watercourse became rapids, which gurgled beneath the frozen surface. After a kilometre of jags and juts, the current broke through its frosted mantle and came together in a foaming, steaming rush that fell between perpendicular granite walls. Martin and Catherine, facing another drop in sixty or seventy metres, motored along the river's green-and-silver-stitched edge and saw the channel widen as it cut due east.

They stopped near the overhang of red-and-beige-streaked ledges, grabbing their packs and strapping on their snowshoes. After a 600-metre walk up the incline, they stood on a triangular plateau that offered a view of the portage beyond the canyon's rim. They stood there, taking turns with the binoculars, scanning the marshes and woods for signs of an unusual snowmobile route.

After an hour Martin spoke. "Nothing. Not a goddamned thing."

5

On the morning after their trip to the canyon, Martin picked up the first glimmer of a clue. Angling between the blue and grey gnarls of granite that twisted into four-sided crags was a frozen stream that opened to the Caniapiscau; it was there, while chopping ice for water, that he crossed paths with a hunter who identified himself as Jared Carbonneau.

Martin eyed the man's load of skinned animals. Caribou had broken away from the northern tracks, Carbonneau told him. They'd headed towards Lac Wakuach, seeking food on the frozen marshes that lay before the hills rolling over to the Goodwood River. After his first sighting, Carbonneau had realized that the stags were leading the rest into spruce and larch seeded into the slopes. He'd been unwilling to fight the incline and had accelerated to a rounded plateau beneath the eastern walls of the Eaton Canyon. From there he'd waited for his shot. At thirty-five metres the animals had presented themselves, trotting towards the chasm and getting penned into the narrow passageway. He'd dropped six.

By the time he'd buried heads and skins under a mound of snow and chopped ice, Carbonneau had known he did not have enough daylight to begin the return trip. So he'd built his campsite near the mouth of the Goodwood, where the portage curved.

"I woke up this morning, and I figured it'd be the easiest way around," he explained to Martin. "The loop past the high rocks and back onto the river, where you can really go fast."

But as daylight had crept over his shoulder and spread its yellow gloss along the ridges, Carbonneau had slowed his snowmobile. Where the path became flat, he'd found broken branches and tumbled rocks. "The trail was really chopped up," he said. "Grooves going back and forth horizontally. Cut one way, then back the other way. Someone deliberately tried to screw it up."

Martin and Catherine found out for themselves when they crossed to the eastern bank of the Goodwood. With his right hand pulling on the steering column and his left hand pushing, Martin had to swing the machine in repeated semicircles to keep the skis on the portage. He slowed the engine and had Catherine lean with him on each swerve, their weight etching a track into the trail.

Martin figured that two machines had caused the damage, racing off the riverbank and entering the portage side by side. They must have stopped and started, taking hard angles to spin figure eights and loops between the green-and-brown, blue-black and grey boulders lining the trail. Martin wound his way towards the twenty-metre-wide ledge that ran between the conflicting slopes, unable to go faster than ten kilometres an hour.

Motoring through a break in the rocks, they climbed to a rounded crest above one of the Goodwood's tributaries.

Martin manoeuvred around a blue-speckled crack and tightly slalomed down to the next stream. Heading southwest, he yanked a hard left away from the water and up a hill of sandstone and shale. After a left-right-right sequence brought him to a line of birch, he correctly guessed that the portage lay after the granite slag, which required yet another right.

Despite his hope, the path continued to show signs of sabotage; the drivers had used their machines to churn up brick-size chunks of ice. Martin's snowmobile still bounced over the bumps while he looked for a spot to zoom off the path and bypass the high granite. The route split after four or five kilometres, and he saw the new tracks Carbonneau had made. He swung east through a line of timber and began yet another climb, traversing the seams of beige sandstone and splashes of rose-tinted iron ore that marked the canyon's eastern rim.

At the top, he drove through fresh snow, picking up scattered caribou prints. The animals had apparently lost their way and panicked when exposed to the wind. Instead of following the tracks, he pulled up to a large boulder and switched off the ignition, then asked Catherine to join him on top of the rock. Pointing, he explained how Carbonneau's trail headed east, while the two drivers who screwed up the portage had broken south.

"If we follow Carbonneau, we'll be going to Lac Wakuach or Lac Dunphy," she said of the hunter's path. "You know that land."

"I'm thinking we should follow it. Take a chance at caribou."

"There's no secret about that direction!" she snapped, then pulled back. "The animals are gone. Your new friend beat us to them."

"I'm not so sure." Martin scanned the valley to their left. "The guys who wrecked the trail went down the Goodwood, right?"

"Everybody goes that way," she answered, pointing to their right. "You've done it yourself a few times, haven't you?"

"Of course."

"But you're not convinced about Carbonneau, are you? I'm telling you he's just a hunter."

"No. I can't take anything for granted." Martin paused. "I don't know if we should go after caribou or after the men."

"Think clearly."

Martin sighed. "I can't."

"What and who are you looking for?" Catherine muffled her voice to blunt the impact of her words.

"I don't know."

Within ten minutes, they turned off the rim and began the gradual easterly descent into the valley and its elliptical groves. Halfway down the slope, they spotted bright splotches of scarlet to the right, about 800 metres from the top of the ridge.

They pulled up to the severed caribou heads and mounds of skin. "I told you," Catherine said, "your man Carbonneau is just a hunter who followed the animals, bagged them, and went home. He had nothing to do with the others."

"The others fucked up the trail, then circled back to the Goodwood, and went straight south," he conceded.

"Just like I said."

I n the early afternoon they reached the Caniapiscau's bend to the north, where the current picked up speed and bubbled through a descending array of L-shaped chutes. Streaked with the brown of sand and pebbles, the water roiled into the western end of the turn, then flowed straight. Martin found a twisting path between the rocks and the rapids to a ridge that opened to a cliff. He accelerated through a fracture of limestone and onto a plateau.

As he hunched forward and throttled the engine to full torque, Catherine tightened her clasp around his midsection and shielded her face behind his shoulders. This forty-kilometres-an-hour speed, she knew, was the first sign that Martin was focusing on the hunt. After the setbacks, dead ends, and unanswered questions of the attack, he'd returned to his original objective — leaving the city behind and coming home to his peninsula.

At last she, too, concentrated on the hunt. The animals needed protection from wind and snow at this time of year. Though they could easily find food on the open streams, they sought water and warmth in the spaces between rocks or screened by brush.

When the channel began to contract and twist around two small islands that ran perpendicular to a chute of fast water, Martin slowed. Cutting a hard left, he steered onto the western shore and looped through the wooded banks to the bottom of the last cascade. After the river straightened, the trees disappeared, replaced by patches of stunted brush skipping the sides of the sharp granite terraces. A gentle bend to the left, and the rocks opened to a small pond, where caribou tracks were clear. Four, maybe five animals had passed between yesterday's moonrise and today's dawn. The animals had dodged in and out of the crags, apparently looking for shelter and a patch of moss, occasionally finding a small cave, but always returning to the Caniapiscau and heading north towards the barrens.

Martin was afraid of travelling too far without enough daylight and thought about turning back to the campsite, but the allure of catching prey was too great. Though the harsh, angular crevasses warned of wolves, he picked up the pace. Within five kilometres, he saw splotches of blood in the snow and immediately recognized the tightly interwoven, crisscrossing prints of an ambush. Catherine was the first to spot four carcasses frozen in a pool of scarlet ice and snow. The work of wolves. They'd immobilized the caribou by mauling their legs, then ripped open their bellies.

6

Madeleine went through Martin's apartment, methodically checking in drawers and closets, examining shelves and cupboards, trying to convince herself that nothing was missing. Hundred-dollar bills were scattered across the floor in the den. She counted the money several times and always tallied $7800, the amount Martin had left behind. His double bed had been tumbled, but the VCR and television were untouched. Lamps, tables, and upholstered chairs had been upended, yet the compact-disc player, tape deck, and speakers had not even been disconnected. Books and magazines lay on the floor beneath posters and pictures that hung undisturbed. Overall, the damage was minimal, and it did indeed appear nothing had been stolen. Obviously the intent had been to make a mess and to intimidate.

And for seventeen hours, it succeeded. Walking from room to room, repeatedly checking the front door and the windows, Madeleine fought confusion, surprise, fear, and fatigue. She tried to think about who might l ave keys to the apartment, but she didn't know enough about Martin's life. She refused to sleep until she'd swept and mopped the floors, dusted shelves, and sponged down the walls, and she decided the intruder had to be someone Martin knew — a business associate, a jilted lover, a skunked partner. Someone had turned on him.

Madeleine assembled and reassembled information, names and dates, places, fragments of conversations and bits of gossip. Catherine had explained how he needed all the side deals to get together enough cash to purchase large quantities of cigarettes and liquor through a pair of Corsican brothers. Once or twice a month, Madeleine would be asked to drop off an envelope to a Chinese importer or hold a small stash of dope — heroin from Lebanon or Pakistan, cocaine from South America — for a quick turnaround. She'd gleaned that most of Martin's business revolved around moving goods through the Mohawk territories and other portions of the United States. She recalled the times he'd been summoned by the Corsicans to meetings about cigarettes and liquor, cash and percentages. After the meeting in October, Catherine had been dispatched on a series of dope deals, gathering a small bundle of cash to be flashed at the next meeting in November, when Martin needed to show his ability to pay for an order of tobacco and liquor. That was when Madeleine had begun to see how the Corsicans floated money in advance of the Mohawks' cigarette deliveries from the United States to a warehouse in Montreal's east end, where they were packed for distribution.

She figured that the Corsicans would never relinquish their control of the trade in and around the city. As Martin had once explained to her, their agreement offered him a bit of room for his side deals and parlays. On occasion, she saw him negotiate approvals and brokerage payments. When a handful of Greek businessmen wanted their own supplier of tobacco and liquor for their restaurants, Martin patched together a deal that included himself, the Mohawks, and one of the Corsicans. He applied the same strategy to convenience-store owners, who were always haggling for better prices. The trick was to bring together the various parties, take a modest fee, and let the others divide the rest.

When Madeleine had expressed her fear of getting caught, Catherine explained that the Corsicans enforced a strict set of territories. The deal allowed Martin and his associates to freelance as long as they did not cross the Corsicans' boundaries.

Madeleine worried about that possibility now. She had little knowledge of his associates and how Martin fit into their business. On the Corsicans' turf — the city — he took the small scores they gave him, and calculating the risks, pieced together larger deals. She understood that the Corsicans allowed him to work the small-time hustles that set him up to turn a profit north of Tadoussac. If he made money on the peninsula, then Martin could dart in and out of this market, staying away from competitors who could easily outmuscle and outspend him.

He had to keep one step ahead of the pace, a tactic that sent him in and out of shipments and deliveries, currency trades, and back-alley transactions. During the past few months as his employee, Madeleine saw how he worked. To protect a price, he changed money from Canadian to American; to support a supplier, he arranged for trucks and drivers; to make a connection, he held dope and home phone numbers. Corsicans, Colombians, Haitians, and Europeans wandered in and out of his apartment, getting word on transit points and travel routes. While Martin laboured long and hard to earn his fees, Madeleine never saw him take a piece that wasn't his. To keep these transactions moving, he used Corsican financing rather than slow things down until he could raise money to buy merchandise and send it to Quebec City. From there it went northeast on credit.

No one else wanted to work that territory.

"Too fucking cold," one of the Corsicans had said at the late-December meeting in Martin's apartment. Studying the maps that covered the wall opposite the full-length windows, they'd discussed the logistics of Martin's trip, the schedule for getting tobacco down the St. Lawrence and across the Saguenay.

That was where they figured Martin would make the play — and Antoine Danielle would bring back the cash. The Corsicans appeared to trust Martin, and they never questioned him about Antoine's reliability. When it had come time for a show of good faith, Martin opened the desk drawer and calmly handed over bricks of greenbacks totalling $23,700.

The Corsicans had then been directed to the hallway, where Martin pulled a cardboard Sony-television box out of a closet. As the men had fingered the elastic-banded piles of Canadian bills, Madeleine and Catherine had exchanged glances, a silent admission that neither had known about these hiding places, that they'd been fooled. For Martin, while disclosing drop points and makeshift safety-deposit boxes, self-storage rentals and strategically placed foot lockers, had often warned them against stashing cash in the apartment.

"Something to rip off," he'd said.

When the Corsicans had left with another $66,800 Canadian, both women had wondered whether his deceptions were a matter of distrust or simply prudent business practice. Perhaps a little of both, but Catherine had taken it personally, initially retreating to a silence broken only by Martin's good cheer. He'd opened beers for three and proposed a toast to their success in arranging credit for the biggest deal of his life. After another round, he'd wandered over to the map, pointing to Natashquan, Alma, Sept-Îles, Baie-Comeau, St-Augustin.

"You never know where you can make money," he'd said. "More than 60,000 cases of cigarettes going this way."

When he first heard the chopper, Martin raised his head from the sleeping bag and strained to listen. Any change in engine speed might mean the cops were revisiting the cabin and picking up a trail that could lead to his tent; in the predawn light, he knew that curls of smoke from the stove could be detected. Unable to discern the chopper's route, he bundled himself into his parka and leggings, untied the canvas opening, and went outside to listen.

The helicopter, it seemed, had swung to the north bank of the Caniapiscau, eclipsing the Gorge des Bas and bypassing the canyon. Still not sighting it, Martin followed the waning groan and tried to convince himself that the officers were chasing a matter that had nothing to do with the cabin fire. As the sound continued to fade, he considered the possibility of the cops' finding the attackers before he did. But then, why would the police be interested? Their job revolved around protecting the dams and dikes, transmission wires and switching stations, crisscrossing the terrain.

Martin's vast network of trade remained invisible to the authorities. They couldn't see the interlocking relationships, let alone the parties' interdependent needs for trade, cash, liquor, tobacco, food, and fuel. Federal and provincial governments, blind to the shadow economy, pumped hundreds of millions of dollars into mines and hydroelectric projects, railways, uranium-exploration sites, lumber camps, defence installations, land-claims negotiations, social-service work, anthropological studies, schools, and band-council programs. Unless the deals had a direct impact on whites or erupted into violence that couldn't be hushed up or contained, they had neither the time nor the desire to unearth the small wheels that greased the bigger ones.

In all his years working in the underground economy, Martin had never been arrested or even interrogated, but he could not let himself get overconfident. His associates in Montreal could easily attract the attention of those task forces and elite units who sought leads on Mohawks and smugglers, tax cheats and mafiosi. Martin reckoned they might have a file on him, perhaps a listing or cross-reference of phone numbers or licence plates. He knew too many crooks to keep himself hidden: the Corsicans, who saw Martin as a bit player, one more hood to offer them the chance to invest and double their money within weeks; the Mohawks, to whom he was a trusted ally in their political schemes; the Greeks and Lebanese, Nigerians and Haitians, for whom he offered reliable transport in and around an underground that expanded and contracted with the hum of a fax or the ring of a cellular phone.

Now as he heard the faint clatter of the chopper returning, Martin figured that the cops had to have some record on him, but nothing that would ever draw their attention. He considered dousing the fire in the stove and waiting for the sound of the helicopter to fade completely.

When Catherine stepped out of the tent, she saw the furrow on his brow. "They're pretty far away," she said. "Sounds like they're going along the north shore of the Caniapiscau. They flew past us."

"I know. I just feel very unlucky. Spooked."

"It hasn't been a good trip."

"No — " he shrugged " — just good business."

The helicopter moved in and out of earshot over the next half hour, but Martin realized that the pilot was concentrating on the wooded hills that rolled northwest of the river. "You're right," he told her. "They don't want us."

She took his hand and led him back into the tent.

Madeleine rolled off the couch and made her way to the window. Watching snow fall in huge wet flakes, she shook and stretched her skinny legs, making the loose blue sweatpants flap. She squatted, straightened, and touched her toes, then tucked in her St. Louis Cardinals T-shirt and circled her arms. She took a few deep breaths and leaned close to the glass. With her index finger, she outlined her reflection, tracing the triangular shape of her cheekbones, the rounded point of her chin. She could see how pale her walnut-shaded complexion had become. She tried some exercise again, but it still didn't restore colour to her cheeks.

At the end of next week, she expected to receive tickets and money from Martin's messenger. Then she could leave and probably meet Martin and Catherine in Schefferville as they moved east. Guessing they were in the cabin at the Gorge des Bas, she believed they would spend a couple of weeks west of the Quebec-Newfoundland border, then head east for the caribou at Lac Joseph, the Rivière George, Ungava, or even the Torngats. If she were to leave now and use her own money, she'd have to burn time. Buy an indirect ticket, go through Quebec City, or Baie-Comeau, stop at Les Escoumins or Betsiamites. Perhaps hide out in a small town like Baie-Trinité or go all the way up to Mignan.

That was the safest way, she told herself. Disappear, hide, give the places she knew her presence might draw attention — Tadoussac or Sept-Îles — a wide berth. Change the locks, secure the apartment, and leave now. Take Martin the warning: someone wants a piece of your operation.

But she'd promised to wait. He'd given her specific conditions and she'd agreed to them. He wanted her to leave at a certain time, perhaps carry a message or bring something. Maybe she was to finish a business deal.

He needed her to stay; the intruders wanted her to leave. Their purpose had been to create fear and show their lack of respect for Martin. Too many variables.

Madeleine wanted to make a fast exit. To cut and run, however, would leave her chasing Martin and Catherine in the midst of their hunt.

What would happen if she went to Schefferville and their plans changed? she asked herself.

Madeleine crossed to the maps on the wall. Taken from the Department of Mines and Energy, the Geological Survey, the Department of Oceans and Fisheries, and the Canadian Armed Forces, they were placed side by side like pieces of a fresco or a stained-glass window. Madeleine studied them. Though the large S-shaped swatches of pink and black stripes outlined tracts of anorthite and granite respectively, she saw the contour of the Caniapiscau and its approach to Gorge des Bas represented as an opening to the scarlet and orange of the Eaton Canyon. Tracing the lines from one map to another, she saw how Martin and Catherine could easily take the river all the way to Kujjuaq, chasing the animals into the barrens the way earlier generations had. Or, if the caribou ran southeast, they could veer off the Caniapiscau and head down the Goodwood into Schefferville.

It was impossible for Madeleine to put together a coherent picture. In the confusing swirl of her situation, the maps were at once familiar and foreign. Memory summoned her childhood trips into the eastern flats across Lac Attikamagen, where lines of spruce and larch provided shelter from the wind: the women and children camping off Lac Tudor or Lac Mina, where her grandmother collected boughs and branches for kindling and smoking meat; saplings securing the tents and poles, and being cut to build platforms for bones and skins — offerings from the hunt; the men, after eight or nine days, setting off for the cliffs overlooking Lac de la Hutte Sauvage or the ridges marking the pathways to Ungava's shore.

When Madeleine's French-speaking father was one of the few Naskapi or Montagnais to work for the Iron Ore Company at Sept-Îles, most of her relatives near Schefferville had not yet lived in a house. Now she was in Montreal, and her job was to wait. If she missed Martin's call, she could screw up his plans, fuck up a deal, leave him without a fallback in case something in the bush went wrong. He always planned for emergencies.

They always happened.

She couldn't leave Montreal now. The break-in was a signal, a code that only Martin could decipher. Instead of interpreting it, she should be protecting his carefully crafted plans by assuring her safety and thwarting another intrusion. She should act with prudence and deliberation, not on impulse, stick to the schedule this time. Heading into the kitchen, she grabbed the phone book. On her third attempt, she found a locksmith who agreed to come in the early afternoon.

When he appeared around one o'clock, she was armed with a fresh pot of coffee and a few pastries — just a new tenant worried about security. She placed a mug and plate on an overturned crate for him and sat in the living room with a book on her lap as he dismantled the doorknob, replaced the lock, and added another. An hour later he was done. She paid in cash.

Madeleine tried the shiny new keys. After they worked twice without a hitch, she put them in her purse and left the apartment. Once on the street, she dropped the old keys into a sewer.

7

The wind changed and began to come from the northeast.
Martin heard a faint crack outside. Perhaps a tree trunk
had broken and crashed into the snow and ice, or perhaps a
boulder had slipped. But the second and third bursts of sound,
coming in rapid succession, were unmistakable.

"Yes," Catherine said when he turned towards her. "It's a
rifle."

The next volley carried a sharp echo.

"At least two guns," he replied, pulling himself closer to the
stove.

Catherine hunched towards the tent opening. Lifting the
flap, she stared into the dark grey sky. "This late and in this
weather." She shook her head in bewilderment. "There's nothing to see, no light, and the clouds aren't going anywhere."

"New storm." He shrugged. "The wind shift will bring wet
air from the ocean."

"More snow." Using her glove as a pot holder, she poured

herself another cup of coffee and gave Martin a refill. "Do you think they're lost?"

"Maybe in trouble." He paused. "Could've been shots to call and respond."

She watched him drink, his brow creased, his eyes slowly closing and opening again. After his second sip, she said, "Did you ever think about leaving me behind?"

He turned to her. "Many, many times." He laughed, his face widening into the shape of a pear. "I always thought it would be easier."

Catherine allowed herself a smile, then sobered. "Now, what do you think?"

He saw she was serious and reined in his amusement. "Do you really want the answer?" He hesitated, then surprised her. "With all that's happened, I feel bad."

"It's not your fault."

"That's not the point." He fidgeted with his cup. "You didn't have to go through this."

Two shots in quick succession interrupted them. To answer Catherine's quizzical expression, he continued, "Chances are someone came across wolves."

She studied his face closely. "Tell me that you're not thinking about someone looking for you."

"These shots?" he asked. "I'm not concerned. Maybe it's a hunting party that split up. Whoever they are, these people have nothing to do with us."

She looked away, watching the coffee swirl in her cup. "You're scared." She took a mouthful.

"In general?" Martin reached for her arm and squeezed. "I'm worried." His eyes told her he would not let an argument begin.

More gunfire sounded. Two shots, the second clearly answering the first, east to west, from jagged peaks to the watercourse.

"They can't be far from each other." He cracked a slight smile. "Just trying to regroup."

She noticed his relief. "Imagine travelling in this weather."

"That's what worries me." He waited a beat. "They have to be on the run or desperate to find their prey. There's no other reason to be out."

Concerned about the wind, Martin secured the tent's corners before bundling himself into his sleeping bag.

Thwap!
  The snapping of the canvas woke him. In the haze of interrupted sleep, he told himself to lie perfectly still. He pictured his moves — a rolling scramble for the knife near his pack, a fast grab for the water, which could be tossed. Staying in here was an advantage. They controlled the outside; he held the inside.

Thwap!

He listened for voices or the crunching of crusted powder beneath the webbing of snowshoes. But there was nothing.

Thwap!

He focused on the poles and crossbeams, relieved that they remained solid. As he thought about a dash for the rifle, Catherine stirred.

"What is it?"

He hushed her. Together they listened.

Thwap!

Martin reached for the lantern. "I don't want to do this, but . . . "

In the half light, she watched him slip out of his sleeping bag and dress without a sound.

Thwap!

He grabbed the flashlight and crouched near the tent opening, trying to gauge where the sound was coming from. Before she could take another breath, Martin pushed himself outside.

She could hear his boots rounding the far corner. She sat up and grabbed the knife. In her mind, she pictured the rifle and shotgun on the left hand side of the sled.

Thwap!

Martin reached the back wall. He took two steps and stopped.
Thwap-thwap!

The canvas wiggled, but the posts and beams held.

She heard his steps come back to the tent opening. He entered, and she heard the snap again.

"The wind clipped a tree," he told her. "It's only about three or four metres tall, and now the top's just hanging there. It keeps hitting the tent. I'll need your help."

The snapping continued, but now it was just another noise. "Some people have all the luck," Catherine muttered.

"Won't be that bad," he tried to sound cheerful. "We've got a couple of hours of wind before it snows. We might get lucky."

"Yeah, right." She looked at him and sighed in resignation. "I'll have to get my ass outside, huh?"

"You hold the light and I'll work the saw," he said. "Might as well take a few of the trees and some bushes to clear out the space while we're at it."

Catherine directed the beam into the tangle of brush. Martin carefully positioned himself so that he could take advantage of the wind's surge. As the chain saw tore through the wood, the severed limbs and branches balanced for a few seconds as if suspended by a cable. Then the gusts took over, twisting the timber away from the tent's far corner. Working with each piece from bottom to top, he cut five lengths, then helped Catherine stack the wood near the front of their camp.

The work energized him. He walked over to the sled and said, "We should protect the supplies."

"Now?"

"It will be easier than when the storm hits."

"Who needs sleep?"

"I don't think we have much choice." He pointed to the groove of stomped snow. "And now we have a pathway around the tent and sled."

She nodded, then scanned the low ceiling of clouds. "Do you think the storm could even slow down the animals and change their course?"

He watched her stare at the sky. "I'm thinking about going

out at daylight just to get an idea of how they're running. The herd could break up, and small groups could take off in any direction."

"I thought you'd want the chance." She followed him to the sled. "You're always looking for an opportunity."

Unsure of the remark's intent, he tried to clarify. "If we can take advantage of the storm — " he paused " — then we should make a move."

Catherine helped him untie the knots and remove the tarp. "I understand."

He glanced at her. "Are you angry about going out?"

"No." She gave a rueful laugh. "Sometimes it's hard to keep up, that's all."

He backed off and returned to their task.

After a few minutes Catherine broke the silence. "The wolves might lead us to the caribou."

Martin was relieved to hear her talk about the hunt instead of the perils of their situation. He proposed securing the camp, then heading north in search of animals. "I'd lay odds that they're running off the bare rocks and looking to cross the Caniapiscau and head into the forest," he said. "Yesterday we were on our way up there."

"Even farther, huh?"

He nodded as they began removing supplies from the sled to make space for hauling their kill. Once the boxes were stacked, they used the shovel and a plastic bucket to dig a half-metre-deep pit to the tent's left. The snow started, big dry flakes, drifting into their faces. Martin and Catherine lined up the gas cans in three rows of five, two rows to be buried in the pit, one to be stashed beside the logs under a blue polyurethane tarp.

To the right, they dug a shallow trench and buried the insulated containers packed with three pounds of packaged meat, five loaves of bread, two pounds of potatoes, four sticks of butter, one pound of cheese, three large onions, a dozen-and-a-half eggs, a cabbage, and a turnip. After covering those foodstuffs, they scooped out an oval to hold one loosely packed box of canned goods and sundries. The sardines, kippers, beans, and corn were separated from the paper napkins, plastic utensils, toothpaste, saddle soap, toilet paper, shaving cream, razor blades, sewing kit, and detergent.

While Catherine went into the tent, Martin directed his attention to the tools. He wrapped them in a canvas bag and tied them to the sled's slats. Doubling a smaller plastic tarp and putting it over the bag, he strapped it down with bungee cords, satisfied that the wrenches would always be at hand. As a final precaution, he checked the spare engine parts kept in the compartment under the seat.

Catherine stepped back outside and asked him about coffee and toast. Her question was hardly out when they were startled by the buzz of engines coming from over the ridge to the southwest, the direction of the burnt cabin. He stopped to listen, leaning forward on the seat of the snowmobile.

"They're on the Caniapiscau," he said. "I don't think they've left it." He wondered if he should ready the shotgun or rifle. He slipped his hand into his pocket and took hold of two cartridges.

A gust of wind brought the sound of the snowmobiles very close.

Catherine figured Martin would grab the shotgun. To her surprise, he waited, his head tilted towards the sound to better gauge their progress. "They're holding a steady pace to the northeast," he said.

Shining the flashlight into his face, Catherine recognized what he intended to do. "You want to go after them, don't you?"

"I just don't want to just stand around," he replied. "At most, they're a couple of kilometres from here. Just over the grove and we'll hit their track."

"You're serious." Fear filled her voice.

"Either we're going to find them or they're going to find us. By the time we get there, we can come up on their backs. They'll be ahead of us and we'll be going downhill."

"Gosh. So it'll just be uphill coming back?" Catherine couldn't hold back her sarcasm.

"It's going to be a quick ride," he insisted. "We'll catch them in a half hour."

"You're crazy."

"There's no choice," Martin said, taking off his snowshoes and hopping onto the snowmobile. Reluctantly Catherine climbed on behind him.

The headlamp cut long, narrow white triangles out of the darkness. Flecked with white from the snow squalls, the illuminated patches could not bend with the river and its irregular banks of stone and sand, brush and silt. From a ridge that followed a marshland and its estuary, Martin and Catherine watched the lamps of two snowmobiles swing towards the woods on the side of the channel to avoid a series of rapids.

The machines were moving at about twenty-five kilometres an hour, Martin guessed. He hit the gas on the Bombardier, pushing it to thirty-five. As Catherine steadied herself by pulling her chest into his back, he eyed the distance between his machine and theirs, estimating it to be about 800 metres.

Though they kept a steady pace, the occupants of the two snowmobiles were obviously not familiar with the terrain. At each bend or jut in the river, the lead driver veered to the left, using his lamp to illuminate the bank and the shape of potential hazards — a cluster of trees or shrubs, a sharply angled line of rocks, a set of rapids.

Gunning his engine and forcing Catherine to clutch and squeeze with her arms and thighs, Martin relished an encounter. They weren't a threat, he told himself.

He closed in and saw the first driver suddenly swerve to the right around the first row of stunted spruce that cut into the channel. But the machine hit a patch of iced silt or stone and spun towards the bank in a series of ovals and figure eights, then flipped into a ditch. The other driver slowed and left the middle of the river.

Aware that his approach would immediately be perceived as hostile, Martin cut his speed and started a wide semicircle.

He guided his machine up the bank, his lamp illuminating the area of the accident. At thirty metres he slowed to a putt-putt, and Catherine let go, swinging her legs to the left side of the chassis and reaching for her snowshoes. She looked over and saw there were three men, not two, and she approached carefully, knowing that a woman might add to their suspicions. She held her flashlight above her head to show she was unarmed. When Martin yelled to them in French, they took a moment before struggling with a response. Then he understood: they were Inuit. As he dismounted and strapped on his shoes, Catherine was already close enough to see that the party was two young men and an elder. Martin switched to English, assuring them of his intent to assist, not harm.

He walked to the rear of the upended machine and paired himself with the driver while Catherine joined the old man on the left side. Martin and his partner pushed up and through the Y-shaped bunch of branches and twigs; Catherine and her partner used the leverage of their combined weight to prevent the chassis from rolling over. Standing to the right of the nose and holding the steering column, the second driver yanked and jerked while checking the skis to make sure they would not catch on the brush or get dented by the jagged edge of a rock. Once the snowmobile was righted, the second driver scooted to the chassis's left side, gripped the handlebars, and vaulted into the seat. After his butt landed with a thud on the vinyl cover, he pulled the throttle. The engine misfired once, then again, and finally started. He steered the machine out and onto the packed powder.

Martin and the two drivers positioned their machines so the beams of the headlamps were directed at the sled, which had twisted to a forty-five-degree angle and left a trail of contents about fifteen metres long. Catherine and the old man focused on the smaller items — knapsacks, spare gloves, an extra pair of boots and liners, a couple of boxes of ammunition, flares, tent poles, a folding spade. The three younger men straightened the sled and went to work collecting the gas and oil cans that were now upside down in the snow.

Martin lined up the fuel on their sled, and the Inuit secured the load. After they hooked on the bungee cords and checked for slack, the three gathered up other spilled supplies — tent canvas, sleeping bags, axes, canned meat and fish, frozen bread, tools. They cut and strung rope through and around each item using a knife and a hatchet. Impressed by their efficiency, Martin figured they must have tilted and tossed, smashed and crashed, their way through many winters. After they'd checked and rechecked the knots, they stood up side by side, and Martin realized they were brothers.

Overall, the accident had done little damage — a few banged-up boxes and cans — but they *had* lost a couple of hours' travel time. They gratefully accepted Martin's invitation to his camp.

Swinging a wide oval to get back into his track, he took them down the middle of the Caniapiscau at twenty kilometres an hour. He found the easy left that wound off the river, then turned uphill towards the tent. The wind was behind them now, and snow blew over their shoulders and streaked into the beams of the headlights. At the ravine they curved through the grove of larch and juniper, their engines groaning, and then they were on the flat. Martin slowed and guided the Inuit through the thickets to the campsite. They pulled up beside the tent.

One of the brothers untied a corner of the tarp on the sled that hadn't turned over. He peeled back the polyurethane, and strapped to the slats were the hooves of four caribou, at least a dozen ice-coated furs, and two beavers. Glancing at the others, he gave a wide smile of satisfaction.

While the Inuit refastened the tarp, Martin stepped into the tent to grab the coffee percolator. He held the flap open for his guests to enter and find spots near the still-smouldering logs, then went out to fill the percolator with snow. Catherine worked the stove, tossing in two logs and adjusting the draft to fan the embers.

It wasn't long before bread was toasting in the cast-iron skillet and the coffee was ready. Martin poured cups for everyone and offered cigarettes. The brothers introduced themselves and their uncle, explaining that they were on the next-to-last leg of a three-week journey. They had left Kujjuaq and kept to the high barrens to the west of the Rivière Koksoak. Instead of turning south and motoring down the Caniapiscau, they'd followed the Rivière-aux-Mélèzes. Crossing the old dogsled paths and portages, they'd dipped south around the rapids and took the ridges to the cliffs overlooking the Rivière Du Gué.

Following these heights to the southwest, they stopped at the Rivière Delay, choosing its wide channel for their trip into the open plain that served as a no-man's land between Inuit and Algonkian hunters. Steering due south into territory that had always been used by the Cree or the northern bands of Montagnais and Naskapi, they crossed below the tree line and reached their goal — the woods and marshlands that offered food and shelter to the dramatically expanded caribou herd. They were unwilling to call attention to their attempts at poaching, so they camped in wooded spots and travelled by night, tracking animals that had found a new abundance of food and water despite the construction of dams and dikes at Fontanges, Brisay, and Caniapiscau.

Twenty years ago, the uncle said, there'd been no need to travel this far from home. Martin nodded, knowing that Inuit, Cree, Montagnais, and Naskapi had kept to their lands for generations, allowing the rivers and streams, woods and barrens, to offer their own cycles of prey. But the demand for hydropower had changed everything. The dams that reversed the flow of the Rivière Caniapiscau in 1984, sending it to drain southwest into James Bay instead of northeast into Ungava Bay, inverted feeding and breeding patterns for much of the wildlife. Newly built reservoirs encouraged caribou to go below the tree line, into marshes and woodlands that proved bountiful enclaves. As the water table rose and enriched the tundra and taiga, clusters of animals broke away from the barrens, and so, instead of waiting for caribou to cross into their territories, hunters were forced to chase beyond the old boundaries.

Until these changes, the wooded turf between Lac Bienville and Lac Néret had been the domain of Cree from Mistassini, Neoskweskau, and Nitchequon. Back then, with the exception of the sacred hunt for the mountain lion, Martin's relatives would not take game from the area west of the Eaton Canyon. As he'd been told repeatedly during his boyhood, everyone had a place. That was how the Algonkian nations showed their respect for one another in this boreal forest, dividing and subdividing responsibilities, bartering and trading harvests of skins, furs, and meats. When the seas froze and salmon, seals, walruses, and whales dwindled, the Inuit hunted to the north, where the Laurentian peneplain opened to a treeless expanse of land. But these territories and hunting grounds no longer existed. Though Martin recognized this as a simple fact of life, his Inuit guests, like so many of the peninsula's residents, were still wrestling with the new reality. They avoided the posts at Mistassini or Neoskweskau, afraid of encountering the Cree. They avoided trading with the merchants at Brisay, Hydro-Québec crews, or other whites, who might pass on word of their successful encroachment into what they still thought of as Cree territory. They never even considered sneaking through the Otish Mountains, down the Péribonca to Lac St-Jean, or down the Manicouagan to Baie-Comeau, where Québécois would pay $100 to $200 for a skin. When Martin spoke of these prices, they merely looked at one another and shrugged.

"That's something for another time," the younger brother said.

Now, the older brother continued, they were content to come through the forest, pick up the Caniapiscau, and make the night run for Kujjuaq. At home, they told Martin, a white trader flew in every two or three weeks, offering $50 for each marten or beaver.

"On our sled," the uncle proudly said, "we have $1000."

8

When the phone rang, Antoine pulled the pillow over his head, then turned sideways to look at the digital clock sitting on the nightstand — 6:36 a.m. He groaned and after the fourth ring snatched up the receiver, cradling it between his shoulder and neck.

"There will be no more chances," said a voice he didn't recognize. It had a high, shrill pitch.

Antoine shook his head, trying to make sense of the words. "What?"

"We know." The voice now dipped to a deeper male register. "We know you served in the forces at Goose Bay."

"Who is this?"

"We've seen you at Tadoussac." The words were spat out. "Sept-Îles, La Romaine, Natashquan."

"So what. Who is this?"

"Even up north, right?"

"Is this a joke?" Antoine sat up and swung his legs over the edge of the bed.

"The Inuit at Kujjuaq, Kangiqusujuaq, and Salluit," the sneering voice continued. "We know."

He remained silent.

"Don't worry, we know you're only the pilot," the voice said. "We know you only make the deliveries and pickups."

"You're crazy."

"Tell Martin Rouleau." A pause. "Tell him we've seen him and we won't give him another chance to steal from us."

Antoine's feet hit the floor angrily, but his response was measured. "What are you talking about?"

"You know."

"I *don't* know." He forced himself not to say more.

"We know he uses your plane and you've flown with him."

Antoine took a moment to figure out what was coming next. "And you want me to give him a message?"

"That's right."

"What's the message?" he asked. "Who's it from?"

"Tell him he's being watched."

"By who?"

"Martin will know."

The line went dead. Antoine sat where he was and scratched his head. Despite the tough tone, the voice had sounded young. He pegged the caller for an inexperienced driver or distributor, probably based in a Montagnais village on the Côte du Nord and eager to do some sort of shakedown or cash in. But the guy didn't know that telephone threats are stupid. He didn't know that businessmen don't fear ghosts.

Antoine was also aware, however, that Martin had won his success through caution and calculation, always alert to the fact that anyone could deliberately unravel a deal or mistakenly reveal information that shouldn't be shared. He knew it was dangerous to consider the call a harmless prank. Though the caller had failed to intimidate him, Antoine wondered how the kid had come by his Cap Rouge phone number. Someone had either betrayed a trust or been careless.

He considered the latter possibility. Maybe someone's frustrations had caused tempers to flare and foolish things to be said. While he couldn't recall any harsh words during recent drops or deliveries, Antoine knew that people on the peninsula lived with narrower margins. The scarcity of money and tight credit increased Martin's power. Besides trading cigarettes and liquor, cash and contraband, he provided opportunities for patronage and, therefore, envy. To some, he was a role model who manipulated white law for gain; to others, he was a crook. To most, he was a mystery, the man nicknamed The Rabbit — here for an hour, then gone.

In a world where there was no spare money, no wage-earning jobs, and nothing to do but hunt or hang around till winter passed, Martin had performed a miracle, structuring a small-scale enterprise that crossed provincial, linguistic, and ethnic boundaries. Whether it was called Quebec or Newfoundland, the land of the Montagnais and Naskapi, Innu and Inuit, this territory was ripe for the underground economy, and it belonged to Martin. In the past eleven years, while government bureaucrats, industrialists, band-council politicians, and lawyers wrangled over land claims and subsidies, mineral rights and timber concessions, Antoine and Martin moved cash and goods, starting with one or two flights every six months, piecing together a run to Kujjuaq with a drop in Mistassini, taking advantage of dam construction and the newly built airstrips. Martin and Antoine were well-known in outposts and depots, construction sites and mobile radar trailers. The caller could have been anyone from anywhere.

Pushing himself to his feet, Antoine crossed to the mirror that hung over the wooden bureau against one wall. He looked into his deeply lined, oblong face and admitted that the episode did tug at him. Had something gone awry? If so, where?

He was stumped by the caller's naïveté and erroneous information. The kid had correctly recited some drop locations, but he wrongly believed that Martin and Antoine would see each other soon and plan a new round of deliveries. Antoine chuckled over that one thing — almost everyone in the business knew that Martin was gone for two to three months. Antoine pulled on jeans and a T-shirt, then went to the kitchen and placed the tin of ground coffee, box of filters, and pot on the counter. As he filled the kettle with water, he envisioned Martin settled in his cabin with Catherine at the Gorge des Bas, each day methodically working north towards Lac Cambrien, where caribou would be running off the barrens and crossing into the woods. That was the plan: follow the Caniapiscau and head for Kujjuaq or break towards Lac de la Hutte Sauvage.

If anything went wrong, Antoine thought, they'd turn south, riding to familiar territory at Schefferville. Martin would be welcome even though he'd had a bitter parting with his family. His father had been one of the first Naskapi to live in town and work for the Iron Ore Company of Canada. Three Rouleau brothers and two sisters attended the church school, then moved away — labourers, a teacher, an engineer, husbands and wives. When the company closed the mine in 1982, Antoine had met Martin's parents; they'd come for a brief visit to Martin's old flat off the boulevard St-Joseph in Dorval. Though they'd never approved of his exploits, Martin refused to back down, insisting he would not make the same compromises his father and brothers had. After an awkward farewell, his mother and father had moved to Sturgeon Falls to live with a younger son, who'd married a white woman and taught school there.

Using the trick Martin had shown him for making good coffee, Antoine added an extra spoonful and a half of the grounds, along with two pinches of cinnamon. He poured the boiling water into the filter and, as the beverage dripped, replayed the phone conversation in his head, convinced there was a piece he hadn't yet understood.

It was when he sat down at the table with a full mug in his hand that Antoine realized that the danger lay in the caller's misguided assumption that Martin was preparing a delivery. If Martin was spotted, then his mysterious adversary would believe he was carrying merchandise and money, a perfect setup. That meant somebody was out there, waiting to ambush him, and scare him off the territory.

Who?

Antoine considered calling the woman staying in Martin's apartment. She might know something. Maybe Martin had carelessly left behind information or some clue.

No. It had never happened. Not once in eleven years. Martin systematically worked his trade, thinking his way thoroughly through each situation. He made a few mistakes and miscalculations, but was rarely without resources and options. He planned for the worst, expected the worst, but rarely encountered it. His flexibility was rooted in his discipline. Patient and tenacious, he took advantage of every shift in wind.

"You can always change directions," he used to tell Antoine, "but you don't have to change your goal."

A t Chute-aux-Granit, Martin and Catherine had a choice. Though the easterlies blew snow in wide, elliptical squalls, the high ground offered a chance to catch a stray animal moving between the trees and cliffs. If they turned to the west with the breeze at their back, then they'd have to follow the streams swirling between the maze of tightly packed poplar and balsam. If they kept going north along the Caniapiscau, they could hold the channel as it cut a valley between 300-metre ridges of yellow- and blue-veined stone.

From their vantage point on the bluff, they decided on the channel, figuring it offered protection from the wind. Though caribou, wolves, beaver, and marten were not in the habit of descending the steep slopes, Martin and Catherine believed the animals eventually would have to come down at least partway, seeking water from one of the unfrozen spots in the many tight switchbacks.

Martin motored off the ridge and approached the first split, then easily wound the Bombardier through the first set of triangular cracks, dipping with the channel, then taking the gentle rise to the terraces that hung over a sharp bend. He studied the oval ledges, knowing he could get turned around once snow covered the machine's track. A route mapped in his mind, he steered through three right-handed arcs away from the rush of water.

The Bombardier entered narrow depressions of stone and grit, and on these iced gravel paths shielded from the wind, Martin slowed to a putt-putt. After a left, right, and left again brought him to another ledge, this one making a slight ascent, the path widened into an oblong plateau, stretching from a strip of pointed shale to a gnarled ridge that went up another 120 metres.

The wind unexpectedly exploded into their faces when they crested the ridge, and they could barely hear the drone of the engine. At twenty kilometres an hour, the chassis shook as the chain churned the granular surface, scooping the powder. *Rat-tat-tat.* At the steep hills between lines of black spruce and stunted alder, the ridge stumbled into the trees and the path curved wide to the right.

Rat-tat-tat. Brrrrraaaaahhhnnng!

Whoa! He yanked to a stop in the middle of the curve, catching sight of a grouse huddled between boughs and needles. Unwilling to shoot, he spun in a fast circle, jolting Catherine and nearly tipping the machine. He raised his arm and she immediately understood: the bird had built a nest. If the surroundings could sustain a grouse and fledglings, there were the possibilities of mammals.

"We're on the right track," he told her.

"For the first time," she shot back, and he laughed.

He turned back around and ploughed into the climb. They hunched over and ducked the wind, their heads and shoulders bobbing and weaving like boxers. It took all Martin's weight to steer and balance; Catherine had to hold on to him with everything she had, yet at the same time allow him the freedom to keep control of the powerful machine. Up and down, grip and release, she told herself, fighting the pain in her arms.

At last they came to the end of the tortuous ridge and took the short, steep path to a narrow plateau, which offered easier passage. With the machine on a steady course, Martin's shoulders and back offered Catherine a solid shield against the squalls that now blew directly at them. He accelerated, hoping to manoeuvre in and out of twisting channels formed by crags and barbed rocks. As they approached the next set of heights, he saw that the left turn swerved to an L-shaped gap. He leaned into the curve and gently steered onto an angled snowdrift. Catching Catherine completely unprepared, he gunned the engine and flew over the three-metre-wide break. When the skis struck and the chassis bounced back on the snow, Catherine gasped. Martin released his grip on the throttle and swung in a semicircle that allowed the machine to come to an easy stop. They shared a laugh.

༄

Antoine picked up his first clue at 9:00 a.m., when one of the Corsicans called.

"Do you know where he is?"

"No, I don't," Antoine replied.

"Someone believes he's going to make another shipment, and they want it stopped," the Corsican said, his voice calm and controlled.

"What makes you think that?" Antoine played dumb.

There was a small chuckle. "I got this crazy phone call."

"When?"

"An hour ago." The Corsican paused. "Maybe two. He wanted part of the action. 'Cut out Martin,' he said."

"How did he know to call you?"

"Haven't a clue."

"Martin doesn't keep a book," Antoine said. "He'd never let anyone know about you. He doesn't keep records that can be found."

"He's smart." Antoine heard the Corsican light a cigarette. "No question about that."

"And loyal."

"I'm not worried about that, either."

"So what's bothering you?" Antoine realized he may not have to reveal anything.

"You still have the money."

Now Antoine allowed himself a chuckle. "We owe you 160 and change, right?"

"That's it." The Corsican paused again. "Someone he knows is turning on him, and they'll find you."

"If I want to be found," Antoine said, boasting. "But I don't want to get lost holding on to something that belongs to you."

"Good."

"How about today?"

The Corsican took his turn at playing the fool. "I didn't expect such quick service."

"It's no problem." Antoine deliberately lowered his voice. "I'm coming your way. How about this afternoon around three?"

"Fine."

"Your place."

Antoine immediately understood that the betrayal came from Montreal. No one outside the city knew about Martin's connections to the syndicate. Along the Côte du Nord and even in Quebec City or the Mohawk territories of Khanawake or Akwesasne, he was perceived as his own man. He never let on about the trades and chores, the obligations and terms of partnerships with Corsican financiers. Such disclosures would demean him in the eyes of his Indian customers.

Martin and Antoine knew their smuggling business required that illusion of independence, and they'd spent years building it, improving it, maintaining it. Now someone wanted to destroy it. Beverly knew their money came from the city, but she was kept in the dark about details and arrangements. Over six years, she'd repeatedly demonstrated her trust and satisfaction. While aggressively pushing on price and delivery schedules, she never showed any signs of discontent, nothing that would hint at a desire to attack. If one of her crew members displayed the least sign of disloyalty, she moved on him. She'd come too far to fuck up.

Antoine focused on two possibilities — the Corsicans or Madeleine, the woman staying in Martin's apartment. If the betrayal was a deliberate act, then he figured it had to be the

Corsicans — they wanted to consolidate or realign their operation. If the betrayal was the result of a mistake or gaffe, then the woman had tripped into a compromising position that had come to the Corsicans' attention. Martin had openly worried about his inability to control Madeleine. He didn't like leaving her in his apartment, but he had no choice. She couldn't be taken on the trip and she knew too much to be cut loose.

Heading for the cardboard boxes stashed in a hallway closet, Antoine wanted to believe that Madeleine had caused this problem — by talking too much, exercising poor judgment. She could be handled, the damage repaired.

A move sanctioned by the Corsicans was different. They knew that cigarette smuggling was a multi-million-dollar business, cash coming and going day and night, crossing provincial and international boundaries, from wire transfers to paper-bag deliveries, from midnight truck runs and airplane drops to motorboats and cargo ships. The network couldn't be broken. There wasn't a piece for Martin and Antoine to call their own, only a sequence of jobs, pickups, and deliveries. Though they'd cornered and laid claim to a certain turf, they needed capital to keep it, and they could never generate enough on their own.

After eleven years of partnership, Martin and Antoine had socked away a few hundred thousand, but it was not even close to the amount needed to buy the huge shipments and maintain aircraft and trucks, drivers and storage space. Antoine knew that their success depended on the Corsicans fronting the cash to buy the cigarettes and liquor, fuel oil and building supplies, that could be dropped into the peninsula.

If the Corsicans had set this up, Antoine reckoned, then they wanted to destroy his partnership with Martin. "They'll ask me to betray him," Antoine muttered to himself.

He stashed $160,000 into an overnight bag and tucked the remaining stacks of money into the false bottom of a worn beige-leather satchel in his closet. Then he washed the mug and coffeepot, wiped the counter, and swept the kitchen floor. After making the bed, he allowed himself to relax, calmed by the cleanliness and order.

Giving the apartment one last look, he put on his fleece-lined shearling jacket, picked up the overnight bag, and left.

He walked the kilometre and a half to the centre of town, where he bought a newspaper and sat in a café to eat an omelette. By the time he returned to the redbrick apartment complex and went around to the back, where his silver-grey Toyota Celica was parked, his nerves had settled. There was no need to re-enter his apartment and fetch the revolver.

"Business," he told himself. "Just business."

I t happened. Martin got turned around and lost the trail. For five kilometres he was on the track of as many as six animals, crisscrossing the rocks, swinging into the groves of larch, then climbing towards the summit. Convinced they were lost and trapped by the jagged walls of stone, he followed the hoofprints from crusts to fresh impressions, from aimless wanderings to deliberate efforts to find shelter from the wind. Near the top of a sharp peak, he saw a couple of wide cavelike crevices in the granite and snaked the machine through them. But the animals were gone. They'd dug their hooves into the brush by the edges of the crevices and climbed over the top.

Catherine knew that clear weather would give them a view through the groves and out into the flat, open marshlands that eventually led to Lac Otelnuk. But the clouds and wind-swirled snow confined any view to the spiked figure eights of the cliffs and trees, ice and snow. And with hardened flakes blowing over the animal tracks, it was impossible for Martin to gauge the time and distance it had taken the caribou to run between gusts and resting stations.

One tight curve looped down into a narrow gorge, where the wind could not enter. Stopping at the rim, Martin saw that the 300-metre path offered a chance to snowshoe through five, possibly six, crevices. He dismounted and stepped into the chest-high snow, pushing himself forward to see into the chasm. At its far end, the tracks split into two of the crevices and followed the bend out.

When he was resettled in the Bombardier, Catherine again tucked herself close behind his body. The snowmobile moved ahead with a muffled groan, the chain crawling over the rim and the skis sliding onto the slope. Pumping his left hand, wrist, and forearm, Martin used the brake to slip forward and jerk, slip and jerk again, then slip some more, as Catherine used her strength to resist gravity's tug. At the bottom of the gorge, she was relieved to take deep breaths of the windless air. But in no time the trail had twisted into yet another set of narrow ascents.

As he climbed the ridge, Catherine looked over his shoulder and saw the first of the animals. They'd wandered away from the protection of timber and shrubs and were now confined to the frozen layers of gneiss and granite folds.

Martin pressed ahead on the machine, forcing the animals into a move. The stag broke sharply to the right and led his herd up a narrow gravel path. Though the caribou initially had traction, they began to stagger and slip when the pebbled cover gave way to iced snow. Martin slowed the machine in an effort to stay parallel. Heading for a ledge that led to a snow-filled flat, he came to a halt, then swung his legs over the chassis. As Catherine slid off the rear and sank into the drift, he grabbed his gun.

At thirty metres he had his best shot, angled to the left as the caribou ran towards a gap in the boulders. The wind erupted a split second before he pulled the trigger. The first shot went wide right, blowing off shards of granite. As the animals jumped for cover and scattered, he made a second and third shot, each succeeding only in picking off corners of stone.

Antoine made the right decision leaving his weapon at home. Though he wasn't frisked, a gun still might have been spotted and would have been considered an act of aggression, which could not go unpunished.

The business was short and simple: the Corsicans no longer trusted Martin, afraid his women would lead him to mistakes or, even worse, greater desires and ambitions. They spoke of women having a knack for turning up in the wrong places. Working a business required reliability and trust, not short cons and quick hustles over dope and credit cards, cash and sex. Apparently the Corsicans were unaware that Martin had taken Catherine with him, leaving only Madeleine behind, and for a moment, Antoine thought of correcting their impression. But he remained quiet as their solution came across the table: he was to take the women home to their reserves and insure they did not return. For this service, his loyalty would not be questioned — and Martin could work his way back into the business. There was no need to hurt nor harm.

Antoine eyed the unopened nylon bag, recognizing the agendas that had now come into conflict. In the short term, the Corsicans were never concerned about money. Only about control. But Antoine and Martin could not afford such a luxury. They had to count the money, make sure the shipments were all there. They had to make a little bit less become a little bit more.

The Corsicans waited. Antoine had to make his move without any trace of calculation or emotion. He acknowledged the problem and the potential for harm; he quietly admitted the carelessness of his partner and promised to resolve the matter so business could continue.

His performance succeeded. One of the brothers pulled the bag off the desk and opened the zipper. Reaching in, he grabbed two bundles of $5000 and tossed them into Antoine's lap.

"We knew this could be worked out," he said. "By coming here now, you've shown us you want to work together."

A few minutes later Antoine sat in his car, driving around Olympic Park, taking the long way to the boulevard Lacordaire. Then he went east to rue Notre-Dame, darting in and out of heavy traffic before pulling into a parking garage off the corner of rues Peel and Maisonneuve. He had a cup of coffee and a Danish at a café, then flagged down a cab and rode to Martin's apartment.

When his key would not fit into the lock on his second attempt, he gave it a shake, assuming the brass grooves were worn with age. After several more attempts, he had to face the fact that the lock and key did not match. He returned to the street and double-checked the address. Again using his downstairs key to gain access to the building, he took the stairs to Martin's floor. He tried the key once more to no avail and began striking the door with his fist and calling Madeleine's name.

For a moment he considered kicking in the door or taking a tire iron to it. But at last he knew there was nothing he could do except leave. He couldn't afford to draw the attention of the neighbours.

9

Martin and Catherine staggered into the tent and dumped their knapsacks against one wall, exhausted from a trip that had begun in darkness and ended in darkness. Martin crouched in front of the stove and raked the ashes for a few embers. There were none. Bare-handed, Catherine stumbled outside to scoop up an armful of juniper and birch logs. Martin joined her, and they needed four trips to build a pile of a dozen logs and kindling near the rear of the stove. Then they knelt shoulder to shoulder before the firebox, each sticking in twigs and boughs. After constructing a loose teepee of sticks, Martin opened a plastic container of kerosene and poured; Catherine struck the match.

For a while, they did nothing but watch the flames and add logs, dripping coal oil on frosted bark. At last Martin filled the kettle with snow and set it to boil. He unwrapped four beef bouillon cubes and placed two in each mug, then poured in the steaming water. She accepted with a nod.

After travelling for sixteen hours, they had nothing to say. His legs hurt from calf to thigh, muscles knotted from the chassis's vibrations. His shoulders and arms were cramped from the exertion of twisting and turning the snowmobile's steering mechanism, and a dull ache encircled his kidneys. For a moment he considered strapping on his snowshoes and walking around the tent to loosen up.

But he knew better. At this stage, a burst of energy was an illusion; he needed warmth and gradual stretching. He moved even closer to the stove, allowing the heat to penetrate his chest and shoulders.

Catherine just wanted to breathe and take long, slow sips of broth. She hurt in almost every joint — elbows, knees, shoulder cuffs, collarbones, the back of her neck. As warmth slowly worked its way through her clothing, she leaned forward, bringing her chest towards her knees and taking deep sighing breaths. Inhale, exhale. Inhale, exhale.

She knew that fatigue could be stored in the recesses of her body, that she needed to float through her exhaustion without sleep. As she bent her body and legs, flexed her arms, and swirled the broth in her cup, Catherine felt she was tucking away the pain and stiffness. Finishing her soup, she saw that Martin had already closed his eyes without getting into the sleeping bag.

After a few minutes Catherine pushed herself out of the tent and dug up a can of sardines. Then she settled before the fire, sliced some bread and placed the open tin on top of the stove. Soon the smell of oil and salt fish undercut that of kerosene. As the water came to a boil again, she remembered her father teaching these cooking tricks to his sons and daughters. Born on the flats between Menihek and Attikamagen, he was pure Naskapi, the son of hunters who worked the terrain around Michikamau. Though they hunted north towards Ungava, they frequently traded south along the Moisie or east near Hamilton Inlet and North-West River. That was how he'd learned of sausage and cornmeal, canned fish and bottled oil, onions and spices that filled the air with their different aromas.

With the blessing of his parents who'd instructed him in the words of the wandering priest, he travelled to the mission at Sept-Îles for Mardi Gras Montagnais. He was fifteen. There, he met a girl who had just completed eight years of church school. With the permission of the elders, she journeyed with him into the bush.

By her sixteenth birthday, she'd given birth to their first son. A daughter followed and then another — Catherine. At that time, railway and mine construction had already passed Lac Ashuanipi. Dynamite and airplanes, work camps and white people, flashed in and out of the land, edging into the forests on the southern lakes of Menihek. While her father had to travel farther north and east — above Lac de la Hutte Sauvage — to find food and game, her mother stayed put. One of the few Indians who could read French, she communicated and traded as the crews pushed closer. She was unfazed by the mechanized tools and the appearance of airplanes and encouraged her husband to make a choice that was rejected by many others: a job with the whites.

Catherine was three and a half, holding her brother's hand, when she first visited the labour camp with its many white men and very few women. Her father slept in a tent and ate food that smelled like sugar and flour and was covered in brown and red sauces. It was the first time she'd ever seen a table and a bed.

For the next ten years, her father split his time between the company complex and what remained of the Naskapi camps. As he worked — digging ditches, hauling wood, clearing rubble from blasts, pounding rails and ties — she shuffled between camps with her mother, older brother, older sister, and two younger sisters. She might sleep in a tent one week and a cabin the next; sometimes she helped her siblings skin animals and move lumber and firewood. Her coat of caribou hide and rabbit fur seemed out of place beside her father's green nylon-and-canvas parka and leggings. He offered company food from cans and cooked over a propane-powered flame; her mother provided meat filled with fat and blood.

Catherine grew to like mashed potatoes. She also liked the teachers who offered warmed applesauce and showed her pictures in books.

When the cold weather arrived, her father took his children into the zigzagging lines of poplar and balsam, up the maroon-stitched ridges once traversed by clusters of caribou and now surveyed by iron-ore prospectors who spoke English and French. By thirteen, Catherine had learned how to shoot and skin, inheriting her father's long legs and his speed on snowshoes. She would race her siblings, and she always won.

To reward her victories, her father prepared sardines and onions with bread and soup.

Ever since, it had been her treat.

The curse came wrapped in two yellow plastic supermarket bags — the crushed pieces of a white plastic dog. Removing the bags from the doorknob, Madeleine thought about reaching into them; she considered throwing them out; she wanted to run. Her right hand fumbled with the new key.

When the door swung open she called into the darkness. "Hello?"

She took a step inside. Her legs tingled, and her chest tightened with each shallow breath. Her eyes moved along the walls, where the illumination from streetlights coming through the windows made grey-black and white bars. She checked each corner, keeping the door open. If she was attacked, she wanted people to know.

"Anybody here?" It was an effort to form words instead of angry grunts and fearful screams. "Don't fuck with me."

She realized that an assailant could easily spring at her from the closets or the kitchen. Leaving the apartment door open, she moved into the kitchen, then reached for the light switch.

The ceiling fixture flicked on. Nothing could be seen except the remnants of her afternoon — the coffeepot half-filled but unplugged on the counter, the white-red-and-yellow

Calgary Flames mug in the stainless-steel sink. Returning the keys to her coat pocket, then placing the plastic bags on the terra-cotta floor, she headed back to the living room and began switching on lamps.

Two magazines remained on the table; one of Martin's books about Louis Joliet was still on the couch. In the den, maps and shelves were intact, the money safely stashed in the drawer. She counted it twice, then checked the closets and the bedroom. Throwing her coat over a chair, she stepped back into the kitchen, grabbed the plastic bags, and headed out to the hallway to heave them in the garbage chute. Then she returned to the apartment, closing and locking the door behind her.

Packing was easy. In one of Martin's closets, she found a tan-and-olive overnight bag, which could be slung from her shoulder, and she threw in jeans and heavy flannel shirts, underwear and two turtlenecks, socks and gloves. There was still plenty of room for things to be added on the road. The difficult choices involved money and schedules, keys and locations. She counted $643 in her wallet. Though she could always work for a couple of hours, Madeleine knew she had to minimize risks.

She had to make a decision about the money in the desk drawer. If she took a little and replaced it, no one would ever know. But it would mean coming back or staying in Montreal, where she'd be spotted and followed, spooked and marked. If she took it all, she would have to find Martin — or disappear. She could go west, hit Toronto or Kingston, Edmonton or Vancouver, maybe south to New York or Philadelphia. Back on the run, stealing short-term security and hoping to find a long-term deal.

"Won't work," she admitted. Betrayal had few rewards.

If she headed east, she'd have only one objective — finding Martin and Catherine. After all, Martin held out the possibility of meeting on the peninsula; he'd offered her the incentive of a ticket and cash if she behaved. But he'd made it clear he had something on that she was to wait for. A simple test of her obedience and reliability, it required patience and self-discipline.

Though a quick departure with his money would obviously break her part of the deal, a face-to-face encounter would give her a chance to explain. Only Martin was smart enough to solve the puzzle, but she doubted her ability to find him. And she was afraid that, by showing up at the wrong time, she'd ruin his moves. Too many people knew her in Sept-Îles and Schefferville, and too many things could happen to Martin and Catherine.

Madeleine had to travel on his time. The plan was not negotiable. Even if she didn't take the money, leaving town and missing his message would force him to assume the worst — especially when he discovered the lock changed. Any move was perilous.

"Some choice," she muttered.

The day-to-day odds favoured taking the money and the next train to Toronto. One scam at a time, her life would bounce its way west or south, but never back to Montreal, Quebec, and the peninsula. No one would find her. She turned to the desk and pulled out the cash.

The $7800 was surprisingly light and portable. She put a rubber band around the bundle of $100 bills and dropped the wad into her purse. After rinsing her mug and cleaning the coffeepot, she shrugged into her three-quarter-length coat of chocolate-coloured leather. Then she turned out the lights, stuck the key beneath the rubber band and, with the travel bag and purse over her shoulder, left the apartment.

Martin opened his eyes, momentarily disoriented. After a moment the situation became clear: he'd been dozing, and Catherine had eaten and left him a sandwich. Now she was dozing. He picked up the sandwich, took a bite, and slowly chewed, the sardines and onions reminding him of their conversations about their fathers.

"They must have known each other," he would insist.

"Yours stayed *north*." Catherine's emphasis would always

make it sound as if Martin's father had never left the bush. "Mine went to the *gulf.*"

"South to civilization — " he would pause for her smile " — right?"

Though her father eventually settled the family near the mission at Sept-Îles, he kept to the land near Lac Petitsikapau, reared by a hunter and his wife who'd refused to accept the book of the itinerant priest. As Martin's father would later explain, he first saw a flying machine in 1939 when engineers and prospectors flew over Lac Petitsikapau. He was five when, with his father and uncles, brothers and cousins, the white-and-silver machine droned over the trees in a series of circles. Scared and excited, bewildered and completely confused, the men pondered and fiercely debated the appearance of metal that behaved like a bird.

It happened again, apparently at random, and the men wanted a deeper meaning. They needed to understand why the machine appeared one day and the next, then vanished until a new cycle of the moon. Everyone knew that white men didn't come at random, especially white men who spoke English, pitched tents, and left again.

When the French-speaking priest appeared, he explained that these whites wanted to take red iron ore out of the ground and send it to Sept-Îles, where it could be shipped to America. A year later, Martin's father accompanied the men on their regular summer journey past Lac Michikamau, and he heard another priest tell of the great war across the ocean. For the first time, the white traders at North-West River spoke of soldiers and construction, flying machines and tractors, front-end loaders and bulldozers. Martin's father saw things during the summer of 1942 he could have never imagined: the earth moved and was replaced by concrete and metal; airplanes jumped through the clouds and gently floated back to earth; green rectangular carriages used their own power to roll across sand and rocks and splash through water.

He knew it all had to be connected. Nothing happened at random.

After the war came to an end, the flights to Petitsikapau resumed. The white men called the place Burnt Creek and set up cabins and tents, labour camps and staging areas. Martin's father recognized some of the equipment and knew the earth would once again be transformed. He was convinced the word of the priest's God was upon the land of the Naskapi.

In the summer of 1950 he took his bride from one of the French-speaking Montagnais clans that came from Natashquan to North-West River. Together they spent their first weeks moving on and off the air base, finding their way through the squatter camp of labourers that became known as Happy Valley. When the season changed into the brief autumn that flares between mid-September and late October, the young couple travelled to the interior, where railroad and mine construction had already begun.

With the aid of his wife, he perfected his French. With the aid of co-workers who were casting aside the languages of Eastern Europe, he pieced together sentences in English.

Husband and wife agreed that their children would go to school and learn the Saviour's word. Martin was born in 1953 after two miscarriages.

From the back seat of a taxi, Madeleine watched the skyscrapers rise into the canyons that had become downtown Montreal. She worked at keeping herself calm — an odd but fitting farewell for a place that provided her with rescue and shelter, opportunity and a few months of relative prosperity. Nothing lasts forever, she joked to herself.

The driver manoeuvred into the right lane so she could step onto the curb of the station hotel. Madeleine reached into her purse and pulled out enough money for the fare and a generous tip. She swung her legs out of the car and stood under the purple canopy, but she felt dizzy and her knees wobbled. The bleating of horns and the groans of car engines stopping and starting overpowered her senses. Which way to go?

The doorman's plush woollen uniform filled her field of vision. He spoke quickly and she could not distinguish the words. He tried again, but she was still unable to respond to his courteous inquiries. She stumbled, the bags sliding off her shoulder and catching in the crook of her arm — the money needed her protection! She felt the doorman grasp her shoulder, his hands helping her straighten her coat and realign the bags. She resisted the impulse to jerk away; she knew he wasn't a threat.

He offered water and a place to sit inside. Instinctively she shook her head and waited for the cold air to clear her head.

"I'm sorry," Madeleine told him. "I just felt so strange."

"No problem, *madame*." He gave a slight nod. "It can happen to anyone."

She used the moment to make sure of her balance. "I'm sorry for inconveniencing you."

"No inconvenience at all." He stepped away.

"Thank you. I was heading for the station."

"Bon voyage."

Gathering strength with each step, she saw her dizzy spell as an omen of danger, and that required another round of thought and calculation. On her way into the *gare centrale*, she replayed her options: the west gave her money and anonymity; the east offered only the difficult task of tracking Martin and Catherine, explaining the break-in, her decision to take the money, and the possibility of screwing up a deal.

In the cavernous waiting area, Madeleine walked closer to the board, pondering the possibilities of Kingston and Toronto, Plattsburgh and Albany, Burlington or Boston, the commuter to Sherbrooke or St-Jérôme. She thought about taking a train and then hopping a bus; she thought about a sleeper and riding into the Rockies. There were too many choices!

She approached the ticket agent and surprised herself. She bought a one-way trip to Quebec City. She had to go east.

10

Antoine left Montreal and drove directly to his apartment to check the satchel of money in the closet. Relieved that nothing had been disturbed, he figured the Corsicans would give him some time before realizing he wasn't cooperating. He knew that the immediate task was to find Martin and Catherine and get them to safety. He took the maps into his bedroom and spread them out on the mattress, lining up their corners, piecing together a picture of the peninsula from the Saguenay to the Atlantic, from Tadoussac to Killinek, Ungava to the Gulf of St. Lawrence.

He thought of flying out in the morning, heading for the dam at Brisay, then taking a forty- to forty-five-degree north-easterly bearing to skip up the Caniapiscau. Past the DuPlanter Spillway, he could easily drop to 1500 metres, low enough to spot the cabin at the Gorge des Bas and fresh snowmobile tracks. If Martin and Catherine had taken off for the caribou-crossing points near Lac Cambrien, Antoine figured he could easily find them.

He traced a route and calculated fuel requirements, reducing mileage and coordinates to a shorthand scribble. Then he took out his arctic parka, thermolene underwear, polypropylene socks, and gloves. With his charts and clothes neatly piled and ready, he wondered how long it would take Martin to work up a response to the moves to oust him. Antoine believed it would be a short trip, assuming Martin would want to return to the city and counter the attack against him.

A second look at the maps and notes, however, gave him a different thought: if they came back defiant, what could they accomplish? Martin was clever enough to fight, but not strong enough to win. As a middleman and deal-maker, he did not have the muscle to back up a direct confrontation. The Corsicans would simply blow him away. Instead of bucking long odds, Antoine reasoned, it might be time to call it quits.

He would have to look straight into Martin's eyes and say, "It's over."

As he lay in bed looking at the ceiling, Antoine imagined the scenario again and again, but never got as far as Martin's reaction.

"After that narrow split, we came so close," Catherine said to Martin when they stepped out of their tent. "Do you think the caribou will still be running that way?"

"To the east." He nodded. "They'll go for the marshlands. But I've been wrong before."

"This time I'll cut you some slack." She paused as he positioned himself to start the Bombardier. "The animals were there."

They made a semicircle and steered into the reddish yellow glitter coming through the trees. Once on the streams that led to the Caniapiscau, Martin pushed faster, taking advantage of the northwest wind that blew from behind. Though clear skies meant greater windchill, it was a chance to make time.

Following Catherine's hunch, he retraced their route of the day before. But instead of struggling with the switchbacks and narrow passages, he zipped into the chasm. He slowed to twenty kilometres an hour, easily negotiating the shifts and turns, pressing through jumbled peaks that began the descent towards Lac Otelnuc and Swampy Bay River. Using the cloudless weather to their advantage, they stopped at a cliff, one of a series, and pulled out binoculars.

Nothing.

Due east, beyond a cluster of rounded granite slabs that checkered an iced plateau, the terrain started its slide into thickly wooded hills of larch and balsam. The absence of tracks forced Martin to consider the possibility of animals holding their ground until the temperature rose. He handed the glasses to Catherine and explained his hunch.

She pointed to a diamond-shaped opening between the slopes. "The new watercourse — from the lake to the river."

Though he took the glasses and focused on the channel, he quickly returned to the machine and putt-putted into a crevice, where they were protected from the wind. He turned off the engine, dismounted, and pulled out the map.

"For me it's completely new territory," he said, feeling the need to explain himself. "I missed the tributary."

She saw the confusion on his face. "It's all right."

"We're behind the heights," he said, not looking up from the map. "Wasn't this the back way?"

"No," she answered. "My father and mother took me up here with relatives, and then we went back east. They would never cross to the Caniapiscau."

"But some of our people would follow the Swampy Bay all the way north." His gloved finger traced the river. "Past the old Fort McKenzie and into the Caniapiscau above Lac Cambrien. That's the back way to Ungava."

"Are you sure?" she asked. "Even though you never travelled this way?"

He shrugged.

Her eyes went back to the map. "It's okay," she said. "Take

your time. We know the lake and the river aren't far, maybe ten kilometres, no more. The animals are always by the water."

Martin was surprised by her desire to keep going in this direction. He studied the map, then outlined his idea of picking up the new watercourse and looping back towards the Eaton Canyon. "How's that?"

She nodded. "Do you think they're running that way?"

"I don't know, but we aren't doing very well up here."

Catherine paused to scan the slope. "I don't think they'll come."

"Not one track."

She was the first to laugh.

For nine kilometres, Martin held the throttle at full speed, until they came upon a tableland that crested to a square peak. From here, Martin and Catherine saw how the ledges and terraces offered a step-by-step descent to the fist-shaped shore of Lac Otelnuc.

But there were no signs of caribou.

They raced across the basin, heading for the continuation of Swampy Bay, then turned south, eager to hit the channel and explore the frozen marshland. Going forty, they bounced and jiggled with the turns, a few sudden stops, and sharp left-rights necessitated by the rapids. Patches of moss and bushes raised their hopes of finding animals in search of food.

On occasion they spotted a cluster of wrens or ptarmigans among the branches. The banks, however, were bare of tracks, and Martin and Catherine grew frustrated, recognizing they'd made the wrong choice at the wrong time: the caribou were running to the north. Perhaps, Martin admitted, it would have been wiser to head for Lac Cambrien, but now they had to go back to camp.

As they turned around, they both understood that their food supplies would limit the amount of hunting that could be done. Despite a full complement of fuel, they had less than six days' provisions. To restock would require a trip to town, and that meant losing at least another day. Martin cursed the reality of having only five hunting days if he wanted to go to Schefferville, four if he chose a bold run to Kujjuaq.

Catherine knew they needed a score — to reverse the trip's bad luck, to add to their cache of food, to boost Martin's confidence, to give them something to share besides the threats. She straightened her body to resist the engine's pull, a move that allowed her head to stay above his shoulders. Determined to improve their trip, she convinced herself she would spot something beyond the banks and in the marshes.

"They had to have been here," she said, her gaze darting to either side. As Martin followed an easterly bend, she pushed herself even farther up. *There!* She pointed to prints slanting into a thicket of alder, two sets forming a path the machine could follow. A tight ninety-degree turn and they were on track. Beyond the doubled lines of brush and branches, the animals had dashed across a tear-shaped pond and onto a bare ridge of grey rock. Trotting up the crusted snow that lay between the points and crags, five, maybe six caribou had found a ledge to take them directly into the trees.

Martin stopped to examine the trail in the grove. Judging from the hardened flakes and bits of ice sitting in the impressions, he was less than three or four kilometres behind his prey. They must be heading for the cliffs, seeking caves and cracks, rather than risk exposure to the wind.

"Is it worth heading them off?" Catherine asked.

"We could go straight to the top," he mused. "But they might not have made it that far."

"Then we work our way down." She ran her fingers inside the print and its crust.

"They're lost." Martin eyed the tracks winding around the trees.

"And tired. Look at the looping trail." She scanned the grove. "They could drift anywhere. We're lucky to have picked them up."

This time he was the first to laugh.

Within an hour, their good fortune had disappeared. Perched on the edge of a red-and-silver-streaked grey cliff, they saw how the animals had vaulted onto serrated rocks beyond a small gulch. The granite on the other side of the gap did not offer a wide enough trail for the machine. Though Martin thought it was possible to slowly carve a trail, the move risked a descent that could easily send them tumbling into one of the many smaller cracks splintered off the main crevasse. They might survive the fall, but the machine would be shattered.

Without speaking, Martin turned the machine around. As soon as he'd cleared the twists leading to the heights, he hit the gas. By the time they'd returned to the watercourse, midafternoon shadows were creeping across the snow, mixing bronze and copper glimmers with black and grey shadows.

Antoine approached the Gorge des Bas and dipped to an altitude of 1250 metres, recalling that he had helped Martin build the cabin under the top layer of stone, sheltered from the wind yet commanding a view of the Caniapiscau. He immediately spotted the heap of ashes and wood splattered across the snow but figured it was one of the handful of burnt-out places he'd seen during his summer trip. Several sets of snowmobile tracks were winding away from the grove and onto the tributaries; a hunter must have fucked up with his stove or kerosene and all the inhabitants had escaped.

Antoine realized his mistake during his second circle of the gorge — there were no other cabins south of the river and west of the rapids. On the northern edge, he saw several encampments perched on the ledges that formed the granite heights. The aerial view gave Antoine a full picture of the snowmobile routes that followed the eastern inclines towards the elbow-shaped bends of the Caniapiscau. At the beginning of fast water, he guided the plane back over the southern shore and went down to 900 metres, training his eyes on the black-ened mound in the clearing.

"It has to be Martin's cabin," he told himself with a wince. "Goddamn."

Positioning the plane above the spruce-lined corridor that carried a stream from the Caniapiscau, he slid to 800 metres. When the forested terrain broke into a cluster of five triangular mounds, he slid to 750, following an L-shaped depression southwest of the cabin's remains. Then he broke to his left, into the southern sky.

He wanted to come directly at the cabin, flying north, then descend along the dogleg that outlined the stream. He spotted the flat patch that had served as the landing strip in September. Pulling back the throttle, he dropped to 650 metres and braced his body for the plane's forward jerk after the engine coughed and the propeller hesitated. The wind exploded from the west and Antoine had to jam the rudder hard right. Then he yanked the flaps up and down, then up again, but could not prevent the gusts from pushing the nose off course as the altimeter read 600 metres.

He figured on two and a half kilometres, his speed falling with his snaps at the throttle. He'd land in staged, choppy drops between bursts of breeze. At 525 metres, he took the hard right needed to bring the plane back to the middle of the stream. Surprised by the ease of this manoeuvre, he brought the nose even farther to the right, which gave him a cushion for the next blast of wind.

At 375 metres, however, he couldn't prevent the plane from drifting too far left. Locked into the angle of this approach, he could only count on a break in the breeze, which would offer a few seconds for a correction. At 300 metres, he cut the throttle for the last time, letting the plane slither between gusts. During a split second of lurching and falling, he regained control by slanting the wing hard right and pointing the nose at the ice.

At 65 metres, he straightened the wing while the breeze slapped the nose up; the landing gear bounced twice. Turning in the direction of a loop of spruce, he found a spot to tie down.

It was one kilometre over the ridge and another three-quarters to the cabin. Holding back an urge to holler their names, Antoine walked into the debris. The rims and webbing of his snowshoes nudged the shards of broken liquor bottles, burnt plastic wrappers of cigarette cartons, the disfigured cans of meat and beans. The devastation stunned him, and he stood beside a splintered piece of plywood listing over two charred beams.

And then it clicked: the stove was gone. Martin and Catherine must have taken it. There weren't any fuel cans either. That meant they had enough to move on. Antoine rushed back to the plane, figuring they'd gone through Schefferville. That was a day's ride, but less than an hour's flight.

II

SHABOGAMO LAKE

11

Madeleine arrived in Quebec City shortly after midnight, treating herself to a taxi and a hotel room off the Grande Allée. She stepped up to the reception desk and tried out her best French — a career woman travelling on business. The clerk slid a registration form across the counter as Madeleine answered his polite questions about the trip and her preference for accommodations — smoking or nonsmoking? Using a name on a credit card picked up in an earlier scam, she filled out the form and followed the bellman to the room on the eighth floor. Once inside, she rolled a two-dollar bill between her fingers and pressed it into his palm.

She locked the door and latched the chain, then hung up her clothes and pulled out the faded T-shirt that served as her nightgown. But Madeleine knew she would not sleep. Despite her fatigue, her mind was buzzing with the journey ahead. She wanted to call Antoine right away. Martin had given her the number in Cap Rouge — a trusted contact in case of emergency.

She fumbled through her purse, and beneath the bundle of money, her wallet, tissues, and makeup, she found the lined, yellow scrap of paper.

Madeleine did not draw any conclusions from the unanswered rings; business or pleasure could easily draw Antoine out at one in the morning. Hanging up, she turned to the window and watched the line of lights marking the drop into the St. Lawrence.

∽

"They weren't here."

The news caused a flash of pain behind his eyes. Antoine got the same answer from each of the men sitting in the band-council office in Kawawachikamach, a newly constructed village fifteen kilometres outside Schefferville. Along with 4144 square kilometres of nearby forest, this territory was now the official homeland of the Naskapi.

"They weren't here."

Finally Antoine snapped in frustration. Convinced the elders were playing a trick on him, he demanded that maps be produced and routes tracked. The older men complied, with no show of emotion. They explained the various ways to approach the Gorge des Bas and said they understood how Martin and Catherine could have travelled down the Goodwood River and entered town. When Antoine pressed, however, the men began to tease him, speaking about dog teams and sleds, portages and rapids, scoffing at snowmobiles that transformed a week's travel into a day's ride.

"They weren't here."

Antoine could not hide his impatience and they continued to mock him. At last someone said, "Maybe they headed for Kujjuaq?"

"That doesn't make sense," Antoine replied. "An experienced man would never go north with no supplies, not when Schefferville was so close."

They laughed, gleeful at seeing the terrain prevail over a

younger man, particularly the son of someone who'd abandoned the bush to work for the machine.

The discussion continued over tea and bread. Men wandered in and out, discussing the abundance of caribou near Lac Cambrien. With harsh winds driving the animals off the barrens, they said, the wooded, rocky shores were the closest havens. Once inside the spiralling groves and busted crags, animals would split into clusters of three or four, running in twisted loops through surrounding streams and then back to the trees and rocks.

If Martin and Catherine were looking for game, the men told Antoine, they'd head north.

"The old route to Fort McKenzie," added one of the oldest, "right up the Swampy Bay River."

Again Antoine went to the maps, tracing the watercourse out of Lac Petitsikapau, through iron-streaked flats and into forest that gave way to a plain of granite and magnetite. He knew that Martin and Catherine wouldn't camp on these lands, but this route led to the Chute-aux-Schistes, where the Caniapiscau cut north of Lac Cambrien. "The back way," he said to the men, "is almost a straight channel to the falls at this point. Does anyone hunt there now?"

"Not anymore," said a stoop-shouldered elder. "But if you're really smart, you can still catch the animals up there. Before they break south and head for the water table, which has been rising ever since they built the dams. It's tricky on a snowmobile, but you can do it on shoes."

Martin was too exhausted to move, but he couldn't sleep. Lying on his back, listening to the canvas flap in the steady northwestern wind, he thought: they could stay and gamble on the trek to Lac Cambrien; they could stay and just turn south when the food ran out; they could take a few days in Schefferville and regroup, then head east, perhaps break for the ocean or Hamilton Inlet, Goose Bay, North-West River.

Indian territory would be a mistake. It carried too many risks, more so when he had Catherine with him, a woman who'd left the peninsula and gone back, then left again, only to return with him and his money. Though he could dodge the questions, others would make up answers that would travel fast. The truth belonged to him and Catherine — and it was no one else's business. For many years, he had kept his secrets. Now, with each swirl of breeze and flutter of canvas, he saw his vulnerability.

He estimated that their food supply was enough for two more runs at the animals. Maybe he'd get a couple of stags, or a stag and a doe. He could work with Catherine to skin the carcasses, gut them, drag them to the sled, and haul them to camp. But each trip would require hundreds of kilometres a day, plus the snowshoe trek into the woods or crags. The new machine could handle the ride; his body could not.

Martin thought about two or three days of rest, then a push on the fourth or fifth. But a mistake or a serious turn in the weather would leave them stranded, low on supplies.

He remembered what his father had told him about 1949, when the men headed north to intercept the caribou that were supposed to run down from the Torngats. They'd gone hundreds of kilometres, too, on snowshoes and with dogs. They'd made camp, all along the Rivière De Pas, waiting and then walking, waiting and walking week after week. Though their food grew scarce, the younger ones pressed on, insisting the hunt could not fail.

The hunters, subsisting on the bits of canned beans, lard, bread, tea, and the few rabbits and ptarmigans they found, grew defiant in the face of their elders, who cautioned against pride and arrogance. While Martin's father was supposed to be loyal to his cousins, friends, and other members of his generation, he had his doubts. The elders had calmly explained that they recognized danger and would not start a fight either with their sons or the midwinter tempests. Though the younger men provoked a bitter split, Martin's father pulled away and stayed behind, waiting out the weather and returning to Lac

Tudor as the others tried to climb the back of the Torngats. On the frigid slopes, two of the younger hunters had died; the others were rescued when soldiers spotted them from an airplane.

Hundreds of kilometres, he had told his son. That year, the provincial government, the Iron Ore Company, the Hudson Bay traders, and the army flew in supplies through Goose Bay. Martin's father was one of the many who travelled to pick up food and clothing. When the government officials began a settlement that would force Naskapi and Montagnais into Sheshashit or Davis Inlet, Martin's father was one of the few dozen who returned to the interior. Following the watersheds beyond Michikamau, he turned north at Lac Petitsikapau and headed up the Goodwood River until he hit the Eaton Canyon.

Within eighteen months, however, he was starving. Unable to find caribou, he took a job, hauling sand, dirt, stone, and cement in wheelbarrows for the white men excavating mines, building a railway and the town that would become Schefferville.

It was another two years before officials had allowed him and his family to live in the work camp.

Though her legs were stiff and pain wrapped her lower back, Catherine wriggled out of her sleeping bag to feed a few logs into the stove. With the kettle in one hand, she untied the tent's flap and stepped out into the dull grey light of an overcast dawn. She gathered snow and ice, then dug into the buried supplies, uncovering the box that held bread and jam.

Back inside, she sat directly in front of the fire and placed the kettle on the stove. Using Martin's hunting knife, she sawed off two thick slices of bread and dropped them into the skillet with a hunk of butter.

She glanced at Martin. He hadn't moved. Watching him sleep, she ate. With this wind, a trip to Lac Cambrien would be impossible. If they took a day off and kept to the woods and heights around the Caniapiscau, they'd have little chance of finding caribou. They didn't even have enough food to sit out two or three days and then travel. They had to go.

She braced herself for another confrontation.

He would argue.

Shortly after dawn, Antoine took off from the old military airstrip at Schefferville, flying northwest over Lac Keating and up the Swampy Bay. At 850 metres, he'd be able to spot anyone who had camped or travelled.

The tracks at Lac Otelnuc were inconclusive. He saw that someone had cut east from the Chute-aux-Granit and spun a few circles and figure eights, then wandered down the Swampy Bay. The party had followed the ridges and the heights, probably looking for animals that had sought shelter from the winds. Then the snowmobile had retreated and returned to the established routes.

Less than 100 kilometres to the north, between the last hooks of the Swampy Bay and the thin, finger-shaped end of Lac Cambrien, caribou were running in bunches along the twisting, snow-covered passageways that angled through the rocks. Today, Antoine thought, a single rifleman could kill two or three dozen.

Despite this bounty, there were no hunters in sight.

Daylight crept into the Upper Town and poked its way down the avenue St-Denis. Madeleine turned the corner and slowly approached the Citadelle. Though the grey stones and buildings blocked most of the wind that whipped off the St. Lawrence, she still hunched her shoulders and stuffed her gloved hands deep into her pockets, giving a few moments' thought to the banners that trumpeted the upcoming winter carnival. Stay here, she told herself, use the car1 work a few tricks, rack up a couple of small scores, an(head east with a few thousand more dollars.

Play and work instead of work and work, she thought; take a few days of luxury and easy tourist money. When Madeleine caught sight of a café, she stepped inside and took a seat in the corner, her back to the wall.

She slipped out of her coat and ordered coffee and a blueberry pastry, watching a small corner of the Quebec morning unfold. Bureaucrats and secretaries, lawyers and labourers, moved in and out of her view, some rushing, some strolling. Madeleine ordered another cup of coffee, savouring the brew and the waitress's attention. She chatted with her, enjoying the young blonde's formal French mannerisms.

Between the bursts of conversation and the demands of other customers, Madeleine's mind drifted to the memory of her church school's pilgrimage to the Cathedral of Ste Anne and the shrine of St Joachim. Pointing to the promontory of Cap Tourmente, the priests had proudly told of monks defying Indians and hiking paths that led to the hills. Madeleine and the other Montagnais girls and boys had chuckled at the thought of seminaked Algonkians watching the robed white men climb the craggy cliffs.

"As a reward for devotion," one priest had said, "the brothers found blueberry bushes growing between the rocks."

Madeleine smiled at the recollection. A few moments later, she paid the bill, said goodbye to the waitress, and went off to buy cold-weather gear. If all went well, she would leave the next morning.

12

"You're kidding, right?" Catherine asked, after a gulp of tea. "No." Martin had just emerged from his sleeping bag. "Why keep going? We're tired and we're running out of food."

She shook her head in disbelief. Having prepared herself for an argument, she had to hold back her agreement. "Do you really want to do this?"

He gave a half-hearted laugh. "It's hard." Martin scrambled for a mug and scooped snow into the percolator. "I don't think it's ever happened to me before."

"Come on." She waited for him to find the coffee. "People go out and they don't get an animal. Happens all the time."

"That's not the problem." The metal had already begun to hiss. "I feel like there's something I haven't done."

"A mistake?"

"No, I could deal with that." Martin finished the coffee preparations and turned his attention to the bread. "I feel like I haven't done enough."

"You're crazy." Catherine shook her head and watched him saw off a thick slice. "Why did you change your mind?"

"We'd have to go out today," he answered, placing the bread in the skillet, which he then put on the stove. "That means making a run for Lac Cambrien. It's too long. For the first time in my life I said to myself, 'I can't take it. I'm too tired.'"

"That's your explanation?"

He didn't answer until his toast was done. "If we had enough food," he said between bites, "I'd wait a few days, rest up, and plan a real trip."

"Take the tents and set up camp?"

He nodded. "The animals have to be running up there."

She shook her head. "So close to the Inuit? Would you work out of Kujjuaq?"

"I've done it before." He paused. "At least deliveries, never hunting."

The coffee was ready by the time he finished his toast. As Martin poured himself a cup, Catherine changed direction. "I'm glad about your decision." She spoke loudly and watched for a reaction, but he just stared into his cup and took a swallow. She tried again. "I'd have been scared to go and I just wouldn't know how to tell you."

Her words made him look into her eyes.

"I'd want to help," she said. She hesitated, worried about presenting herself as weak. "I'd also be afraid you'd do this alone."

"It's the fire," he said. "It's the smoke and the smell. It won't go away. It's right there." Martin held his hand directly in front of his nose.

"I know." She grabbed his fingers. "I couldn't see all of what happened, just a glimpse of the helmet. Nothing more."

"You didn't have much chance to see." He watched his fingers in hers. "There wasn't any time to do anything but get out."

Her face fell. "I keep hearing the window being shattered."

"They could have set the fire first." He pulled his hand away and touched her chin. "They saw you and ran away. You scared them."

"I don't think so." Catherine let out a nervous laugh.

"It's the only way that makes sense."

Though he scooted closer, she recognized the distance between them. "It all just happened."

They were still talking about the fire twenty minutes later as he stepped outside to toss more snow into the percolator and check the weather. "It's such a blur," she said. "I wish I knew why they did it."

"Or who," he added.

"Is that a problem?"

"It's *the* problem." He nodded. "Someone tried to kill us, and I'd like to know who."

"So you've changed your mind." She picked up the jar of jam. "At first you said they didn't want to kill us. Now you say they did. Why?"

"I keep thinking about it," he replied. "The only reason to go all this way is to find us, then finish us. Don't you wonder who came after us?"

"I told you before, it doesn't matter." She took a moment to cut a thin corner of bread. "But you're scared, right?"

He did not expect the accusation.

"You don't know who they are," she continued. "You don't know where they are. You couldn't identify them even if they were right in front of you. Scares the shit out of you, right? It would me."

Martin lowered his gaze, refusing to argue.

Instead of relishing her victory, Catherine ate her toast and backed off. "From the beginning you were right about one thing. We were followed because everybody in the business knew. It was easy to find us."

"Do you think it was Antoine?"

His question startled her. "No." She was firm. "No one that close to you."

"Beverly?"

She shook her head. "As you would say, no percentage." She paused. "Beverly has a good business because of you. Without your connection, she's lost."

"Madeleine?" he asked, only to answer his own question. "She's careless and it's possible. But who from her crowd would take the trouble and expense to come out here?"

"The attackers had to be familiar with the peninsula," Catherine said. "They had to know the approach. They had to have the skill with their machines."

"I'm sure they were hired." Martin stared into his coffee. "They were paid part in advance and just went out into the bush. To them, it didn't matter if they truly finished the job or not. They had some money, torched the place, and went off to collect the rest."

"That's why they couldn't have come from this area. They had to have come from another part of the peninsula." She used her finger to emphasize the point. "Outsiders paid by whites."

He took several moments to follow her logic to a conclusion. "You think the Corsicans want me dead? They'd pay."

"To them," Catherine said with complete assurance, "you're just an Indian."

"They need me."

"Are you sure?"

"I know the territory and I've worked with them for so long . . . " Martin's voice dropped to a whisper, as if he understood the foolishness of his position.

"There are others."

"I should have seen that the moment the fire happened."

Catherine forced a smile. "You didn't want to see."

All morning Martin's mind raced. He pictured the back rooms off the boulevard Métropolitain, the Corsicans talking over a plan, tossing around a few numbers, checking a map. They'd mention their years of working with him, the jams and close calls, his proved record of deliveries and pickups: $35,000 a day, 200 grand a drop, half the load in half the night. His work added up. Yet they would cast the account aside. Somehow encourage someone else to take over. A Montagnais from the Côte du Nord? An Innu from Sheshashit? They didn't care; smuggling was an equal-opportunity enterprise. As long as the bill got paid, a new guy got his chance. Martin recognized that this part of the business was not personal, just arrangements and timing, counting and sorting. He expected loyalty, yet he knew that success demanded the ability to contest an established trader.

Life comes around.

After all these years, he figured, the Corsicans had grown tired of him taking over the schedule. They still determined the prices and worked the splits coming out of warehouses in Montreal, but he set the dates and times, the drop points and transports. His rival must have offered a deal that would split the Tadoussac to Natashquan routes from the Belle Isle to Nain deliveries, destroying his ability to control an inventory. Martin saw the Corsicans giving up a little cash to strengthen their position: throw out the old, bring in the new.

The smart money would bet on Montagnais and Innu partnerships dividing the peninsula. One working out of Sept-Îles, the other out of Goose Bay, they could cut the drop at Tadoussac and streamline deliveries. As more merchandise from the States came into Montreal, the Corsicans could sell direct and move without interference. Despite their peaceful relations and his diligent handling of cash, Martin could see that he stood in their way. He wanted his turf on his terms; they wanted obedience.

After all these years of waiting them out, accepting their terms but delivering on his timetable, they had caught up with him, finding the time and the place to attack. Like good hunters, they were patient — waiting until their prey was backed into a corner.

Did the Corsicans think he'd died in the fire? Letting himself chuckle over the possibility, he tried to be methodical. Would his assailants slip into Schefferville on the way to collect?

Did they come from the northwest?

Were they headed east? Or south to the Côte du Nord?

He'd pondered these questions hundreds of times, but they took on a new meaning when connected to money from Montreal. Logic dictated that he think cautiously and behave prudently, but Martin's instinct had locked on the certainty of a few young men from Sept-Îles or Goose Bay finding the Corsicans and flexing their muscles. Now Martin wanted to find them. He wanted authority; he wanted the chance to redeem this trip. He pictured the charred cabin, and for a moment could almost smell the kerosene and the burnt asphalt.

Stepping outside and strapping on his snowshoes, he walked to the top of the gulley, where he could see the triangular cliffs that opened to the Gorge des Bas. Against the dull afternoon sky, the black-speckled rocks had none of their usual sparkling riffs of silver. Martin studied how the pathways forked towards the Caniapiscau, and suddenly he knew his assailants would have left the river, disappeared from the scene of the crime.

They'd have had to stop for the night, but minimize their risk of disclosure. With cash in their pockets, they could have afforded a night at Schefferville's Hotel Montagnais, keeping to the centre of town and out of the reserves at Matimekosh and Kawawachikamach. If they were smart, they'd have had a good dinner, some beer, a decent night's sleep. If they were stupid, they'd have sat up late in the bar, buying drinks, taking their chances with women.

There could be a trail.

They wouldn't have stayed long, maybe two nights. If Martin guessed right, they'd pulled out along the railway tracks, the spur a perfect highway for snowmobiles. After going south along Menihek, they would have turned at Esker, where the federal and provincial governments had carved out a gravel roadbed that ran 300 kilometres east through the giant hydroelectric dam at Churchill Falls and on to Goose Bay.

It would make sense to disappear. No one would've suspected them of travelling this far.

Martin saw them as younger men, eager to cooperate and

send tobacco and liquor directly into the peninsula. Instead of remote drops, airstrips, middlemen at each reserve, and distributors, the Corsicans would rely on larger areas for landings, using the concrete runways at Sept-Îles or Goose Bay. The Côte du Nord and Hamilton Inlet presented the best opportunities for merchandise to be taken to small warehouses and then broken down for quick distribution.

What route had his attackers taken to his cabin? He thought about them heading south for Sept-Îles, but figured his place on the Gorge des Bas was too far and too remote for them to go that way; they wouldn't have had the patience. No, it was easier to come straight across the peninsula from Goose Bay or Hamilton Inlet, using the roadbed for the Trans-Labrador Highway and then following the lakes and rivers, hopping their way to the Caniapiscau Reservoir. From there they'd be in position to approach the cabin.

They should have killed me, he told himself. For the first time since the fire, a smile crossed his face when he thought about the possibility of death.

"Who do you hope to find?" Catherine asked as he outlined his plan for leaving the next morning and heading for Schefferville. "What do they look like? Are they tall or short? Innu or Montagnais? Whites, maybe?"

He shook his head, knowing she had the weight of reason. "It's time for us to make a move, take a risk. I don't have clues."

"So you go on hunches." She felt tricked. His choice to back off the hunt was merely a cover for his decision to chase the attackers. "I thought we weren't going to do this. It's stupid."

"We can't just go into town and stock up." He jabbed at the beans and then tapped the wooden spoon against the pot.

"I still think we have to go back to Schefferville and wait for an opening."

"I can't do that." He was adamant. "*You* might be safe there. *I'm* not."

"No one'll hurt you."

"That's not the problem." He held his growing anger in check. "People will figure me out. They'll remember."

"We have to be safe. That's my first concern."

"Mine —" he paused to break his yolks and mash the beans and eggs together "— is to strike back."

Catherine took the knife and worked on the heel of the bread. "At least you're being honest."

"I want to take a run at them."

"But who are they?" She refused to concede. "You might never know. Think about that. Where do you find them?"

"The east."

"How do you know?"

"I can't tell you," Martin forced a laugh, then quickly sobered. "All I can say is that I'm sure. It's the only way that makes sense. From Goose Bay, a guy could easily fly into Montreal, make his pitch and fly back. A young man with ambition could make this move."

She watched his face, but his eyes darted away. "You're trying to convince yourself," Catherine said, "not me."

After the argument came the compromise, deceptively simple and clearly indecisive. They agreed to use the rest of the afternoon and evening to pack, preparing for departure shortly after daybreak; there was no agreement on the length of their stay in Schefferville. They uncovered the fuel, lined up the canisters on the back of the sled, and tied them down. Arranging the food boxes and containers in a square on one side of the sled, they cleared space on the other for the barrel and stovepipe, sleeping gear and knapsacks. As always, the front was reserved for the tools, in case of a breakdown.

While Martin slept, Catherine tossed, sensing they were about to embark on two separate journeys. To restore his belief in himself, Martin needed to retaliate against his attackers, even if he didn't know who they were. He had to regain his honour and self-esteem. That version of the trip was about him; her version was about *them*.

Knowing that so much of his life had been spent building this business, Catherine understood that he found his identity by competing against whites and other Indians. She had hoped this trip would allow them the chance to break out of the smuggling and petty crime that had become their lives, but she knew he was not ready. He still needed to prove himself.

Catherine listened to Martin's slow, even breathing. She remembered his tales about growing up in Schefferville — his ability to con the priests, his boasts about his speed on skates and snowshoes. When the school or the Iron Ore Company sponsored the races or hockey games between whites and Indians, everyone waited for Martin to disclose the events he'd compete in — against both adults and his peers. Usually he gave his opponents a head start.

On skates he jumped barrels and played ball or joined the miners at the rink, using his explosive speed and youth to score five or six goals a game. Even the priest bet on him and shared his winnings. At times he played the afternoon game, which followed first shift, then went home, ate dinner, and came back to wait for the match that began after second shift. That was when he'd had his first beer and whisky. The boys from Newfoundland — Gander and Gambo, Lewisporte and Leamington — loved their hooch, and they insisted that the team's star come along to their club. Bit by bit, Martin learned their Scottish and Irish brogues.

As Martin told it, he was approached by other Montagnais and Naskapi, offered money to sneak a bottle or buy some brew. While he learned the hard way to nurse his drinks and pace himself, he found it easy to persuade the tipsy miners to let him slip out with a flask in his pack or a few bottles of beer tucked into the pockets of his parka. To the Montagnais and Naskapi men, he served as a courier.

Though the alcohol and tobacco transactions remained undercover, he used his reputation and goodwill to bring Naskapi and Montagnais into the company stores and supply depots.

With a wink and sometimes a little extra cash — or the promise of a huge freshwater trout, caribou flank, or marten skin — Martin and his friends bartered for gasoline or diesel oil, fan belts and distributor caps, spark plugs and batteries. And then there were deals for wrenches and hammers, shovels and picks, lumber and rope.

It was the only way to get things done, he'd told Catherine, the only way.

13

Madeleine took most of the day to finish. Going from department stores to sporting-goods shops, she eyed dresses and blouses, but passed them up for a sweater, flannel-lined denim shirt, two turtlenecks, and some underwear. At a surplus merchant near the Lower Town, she bought a military-issue arctic parka, gloves and hat, then returned to the hotel to drop off her purchases and play a hunch. In the fading glare of the late-afternoon sun, she hailed a taxi and rode to the airport. With an offer of a fast $150, she spoke to the pilots heading up the Côte du Nord, looking for someone to take her to Tadoussac. Once on the Labrador peninsula, she would take a bus to Sept-Îles. Though none of the pilots had planned to stop, a few were willing to rearrange their flight plans, liking the cash and the bonus of the company of a young woman. Within an hour, a firm deal had been struck. Departure time was 7:15 a.m.

Madeleine packed, after dinner in the hotel restaurant, stuffing her leather coat in the bottom of Martin's bag. She placed her folded skirt, blouse, and sweater on top of the coat, then tucked her high-heeled boots into the corner. Filling the rest of the suitcase with her new possessions, she set aside one pair of long underwear, leggings, and a turtleneck. The parka was laid out on the desk. She crawled under the covers. Less than an hour of television took her into a dreamless sleep, and she awakened to the front desk ringing her phone at 5:45 a.m.

Snow was falling sullenly as the taxi took her to the airport hangar, where the pilot stood waiting, dressed in his drab blue flight suit and grease-stained Nordiques cap. They walked out to the Cessna, and he stashed her bag to the right of the cargo door, then assisted her into the copilot's seat. Then he went back inside for a printout of weather conditions and the latest flight paths. Madeleine watched the fuel truck wind around the closest engine and stop directly in front of the cockpit. As two men arranged the connection, the man holding the nozzle slipped and fuel splashed onto the ground. She stifled a laugh.

When the pumping began, the pilot stepped out of the hangar and spent a few minutes chatting with the fuel-delivery crew. Then he climbed into the seat beside Madeleine, shaking his head, a few snowflakes still sticking to the bill of his cap.

"What a life," he grinned.

"You should have seen them," Madeleine said.

"No," he returned with a broader grin. "I'm glad I didn't." Pulling a rumpled red bandana from his chest pocket, he wiped his face, then grabbed a pencil. He unfolded the maps around his seat and showed Madeleine the flight route.

He put on his headset and began the chatter that would eventually clear them for takeoff. He spoke and flicked a few switches, then the engine coughed a couple of times, and the propeller began to rotate. Once the blades were in their blurring spin, he slid his headset off his ears. "Just don't touch the dials," he told her, "and relax."

She found his candour soothing. "I promise," she said.

Antoine figured his only move now was to return to his apartment and wait for a call from Martin. If there was trouble, the phone would ring; if everything went according to plan, they would meet in April.

Cutting a wide, sweeping arc that took him over the Monts Otish, he wondered about the future of his business. Though the Corsicans made it clear they wanted him to fly their merchandise, he would not betray his partner. He and Martin had found each other at the beginning, when the alternatives were going back to the reserves, accepting band-council jobs, or rotting in the cities. At first a life of petty crime challenged them; then the money gave them a heady illusion of power when they flew into Tadoussac or the territories.

Though the plane provided Antoine with a cover, he understood the need for Martin to reveal as little as possible. For the first two or three years, they'd claimed he was Iroquois, Algonkian, Cree, or Ojibway, anything to confuse his identity and add to his mystery. They floated the nickname The Rabbit, and it worked. But the business had its own logic, which neither Martin or Antoine could anticipate. By the fifth or sixth year, when they'd included runs to the Inuit in Ungava, a drop at Nain, and a stop or two at Goose Bay, they'd realized that their trade depended on their ability to move cash, not barter cigarettes and alcohol, building supplies and tools. As Antoine used to say to Martin, smugglers had become bankers. Boxes stuffed with hundreds and fifties frequently found a place in Antoine's closet. The two of them established themselves as trustworthy and reliable, but they always struggled with schedules. As the pilot, Antoine understood the peninsula had its own rhythm, and weather patterns that attacked in ferocious staccato storms that could either blow away in a few hours or stay for days.

In the summer and autumn, the Corsicans could easily put two or three million dollars' worth of merchandise in his plane for twenty to twenty-five drops. Martin arranged the collections, but his timing rarely satisfied the Corsicans. They wanted a week; he gave them ten days. When they explained that their profits depended on their ability to reinvest cash from one day to the next, Martin never argued. The silent Indian unnerved them.

Everyone knew that the cigarette-and-liquor business offered investors a chance to double their money, wash it, and change it from Canadian to American. Antoine and Martin never messed with the splits, expressing satisfaction with their take as long as they had the freedom to work as many deals as possible. Since the Corsicans rented their services, Antoine and Martin insisted they were not bound by exclusivity and worked side jobs that brought merchandise into Montreal and out to customers in St-Jérôme, Joliette, Châteauguay, L'Épiphanie, Mont-Rolland. In the past two years, they'd even found deals in the city, and the women had helped on the streets.

At times Martin had speculated about breaking away, making his own moves without the Corsicans. But he knew it would never work. The need for cash and credit kept him connected. The Corsicans were the real bankers and financiers. Though Martin and Antoine handled sums once beyond their imaginations, their power had actually decreased. They had become richer and weaker.

Approaching the airport outside Quebec City, Antoine's plane locked onto its descent and slipped below the mist. He cut the speed and pulled up the flaps, letting the Piper down, the wheels skidding a bit when they struck the wet runway. Within an hour, he was back in his Cap Rouge apartment, making a pot of coffee and wondering about his next move.

Halfway through rapids, where swirls of water steamed through holes of ice, Martin and Catherine were surprised by the approach of three Montagnais men, a woman, and two children on three machines. Taking a hard left away from the stream, they met in a crevasse and spent fifteen minutes discussing directions and weather conditions, trails and animal sightings. Martin knew he was going uphill, heading for the watershed that marked the height of land separating Newfoundland from Quebec. When he asked about the Goodwood and its sharp bend to the east, the travellers encouraged him to use the portage for ten or so kilometres, then watch for the blue-brown boulders beneath three rose-streaked granite cliffs. In the midday sun, they said, a pink halo would surround these rocks. That was the shortcut across the border.

In return, Martin employed elaborate hand gestures to illustrate the zigzagging cuts and hairpin curves of the route he and Catherine had just completed. Telling the travellers to keep on the river and avoid the hills, he described the spirals that would take them to the Caniapiscau and warned them they would have to go farther north to find caribou.

After parting, Martin heeded their advice. Although there were snowmobile tracks on the channel, he veered into the drifts, slipping between spruce and putt-putting up a steep hill that flattened to a thick grove. A slow semicircle took them back to the Goodwood River, which opened to a looping left-handed curve. Martin followed a string of islands and swept into a crescent-shaped basin. There, he gunned the engine, racing into the wind gusting over the western ridges and kicking up swirls of hardened snow. He turned southward and aimed for the barren heights: on the other side, where Quebec officially ended and Labrador officially began, the mining companies had cleared a roadbed that ran straight into Schefferville.

Madeleine stared down at the basilica at Ste-Anne-de-Beaupré, remembering the lessons of nuns and priests who took young Montagnais boys and girls from their classroom in Sept-Îles to the altar of miracles. Each year they boarded a dented school bus and rumbled down the Côte du

Nord, spending a night at Tadoussac, then crossing the Saguenay in the morning and finishing the trip by afternoon. From the air she could see how the two grey steeples rose over the ancient pines and dwarfed the village's grid of white clapboard houses.

She pictured the gaunt, balding face of Père Simon, the priest who told the same stories on every pilgrimage. And each year she would return to Sept-Îles, forced to tell her mother and father every detail of the trip. Madeleine was the daughter of parents born into the church, whose ancestors had settled near the seventeenth-century mission. She was expected to know the Saviour's work and respect His servants; they taught her how to read and write, how to harness the raw power of Indian life and bring it to virtue. In Madeleine's memory, faith and piety filled the three-room shingled house her father had built with the help of missionaries.

When the Iron Ore Company needed the land east of the village to make room for the railway tracks and switching yards, the priests found the family a new plot on the outskirts of town, where other Montagnais were being settled. As extra compensation, the monsignor pressed the foreman to hire her father. Within a year, the company took him off the local crew and reassigned him to runs as far as Wabush and Schefferville. He earned more money, but his new duties required his absence for several days each week. During the winters, when weather erupted into its vicious cycles of wind, snow and ice, Madeleine's mother kept a vigil for her husband, praying for his safety as she stood before two postcards leaning against a candle lit below the frosted windowsill. The picture on one showed the basilica's exterior, its spires glossed by the brilliant sunshine of a summer day; the picture on the second was a close-up of a crucifix carved into one of the basilica's many altars.

At Baie St-Paul, the valley opened wide. Lush with pines and fir, aspen and willows, the slopes were covered in snow, which the wind blew in swirls. Madeleine focused on the Rivière du Gouffre as it emptied into the St. Lawrence. The pilot tried to dodge the gusts by thrusting the plane's nose into the first layer of clouds.

For a moment Madeleine's entire world was wrapped in a shroud of white. Then the pilot cut to the south, buzzing over the strait that separated the six-street village of St-Jospeh-de-la-Rive from the hamlet of St-Bernard of the Îles-aux-Cordes. She remembered how the priests taught her that Cartier believed this point to be the border between the Kingdom of Hochelaga and its great river of Canada, and the Kingdom of Saguenay, with its mystical riches, including what the Algonkians once called *cagnitzidete*, the reddish dust that could be smelted into metal.

As the plane swept back towards the mainland, she spotted the streaks of iron ore pleated into the rocks that formed the gorge at Les Eboulements. The plane began to shake, and she laughed like a kid on a roller coaster. The pilot banked a quick circle over the foaming chutes and gave her the thrill one more time.

The fun, however, was short-lived. Between Ste-Irenée and Pointe-au-Pic, Madeleine watched the crusted flakes strike the windshield. As the plane bounced left and right, she knew that the harsh winter weather of home lay ahead. The snow turned to hail at St-Fidèle, and the pilot broke his course, girding in over the continent and climbing above the forest. With a cockeyed grid of hunting paths and logging roads pointing the way, he crisscrossed the rectangular pine groves, cut and regrown, recut and rematuring.

Madeleine wasn't fooled by the patch of fair weather near St-Siméon, where the pilot returned to the river and climbed even higher. The smooth ride offered a brief respite, but the sight of granite blocks forced her to face the reality of her return. There was no plan, no set of facts or certainty to guide her. Like the slabs of stone that jumped and cracked at irregular intervals, she saw herself skipping from one point to the next. She had no other choice. Near Baie-des-Rochers, the clouds returned, bringing snow.

At the Rivière Saguenay, the elements grew stronger. As the plane began its descent, the wind shot a squall of ice chips over the cliffs. Surprised, the pilot broke off his angle, hooking around the wharf at Tadoussac. Once he spotted the airstrip, his hands tightened their grip on the controls and the plane shook hard before settling into a rocking left-right motion. When Madeleine opened her eyes, the plane's nose was pointed down the middle of the runway.

The pilot helped her out. She took a moment to walk around the hangar and scan the terrain. Feathered between the granite bluffs that served as the natural boundary of the Labrador peninsula, the uneven lines of stunted spruce and fir caught the snow and hailstones with a whisper: *tsssss-sssss-stip, tsssss-ssss-stip.*

Madeleine knew she was on her way home.

The call woke Antoine from a nap. When he heard Martin's voice, he broke into a deep belly laugh. They joked about almost meeting each other in Schefferville, then swapped a little information about the Corsicans and the fire on the Gorge des Bas. Instead of piecing it together over the phone, they agreed to meet in Labrador City, where they could rent hotel rooms and fade into the activity of mining-town life.

An hour and a half later, Madeleine called. Antoine listened carefully, took her number at the hotel in Tadoussac, and promised to get back. Then he called Martin.

"It's fucking crazy," Antoine declared.

"But it also makes sense."

"Do you want to call her?"

"I probably should," Martin answered. "Do you mind if she meets us?"

"No."

"I'll make the call now."

"They want you out," Antoine warned, "real fast."

"No," Martin shot back. "They wanted me to die up here, where it couldn't be traced."

14

At 8:30 p.m. the streets of Schefferville were deserted. Through the abandoned hulks of mine buildings, crushers, and screening facilities that dwarfed streets laid out in neat rectangles, Martin could still see the tents and work camps, the corrugated metal quonset huts, the scuffed and scarred fuselages of the four-engine military transport planes. As he walked the paths of his younger days, he easily summoned an image of the flats and marshlands where tractors perpetually churned and bulldozers scooped out the wetland, stripping away the sediment streaked with iron ore. He remembered how the morning sun on clear winter days turned these streaks into rose-tinted shafts that sparkled with ice.

To reach school, he'd had to leave the shack built by his father and cross the work camps, where he'd heard the foreman and labourers speak of the need for volunteers to build a new mine below Shabogamo Lake. At the train depot or the airstrip, engineers and scientists kept coming and going with reports and maps of ore concentrations and rock formations, topographical surveys, and hydrological patterns west of Ashuanipi. While one town was being built, another was being planned. All of a sudden Martin had heard his father speak of a place called Labrador.

At five years old, he didn't understand why the Naskapi worshipped in English with the whites at the stone chapel dedicated to St. Paul, and the Montagnais crowded into the clapboard Church of Mary Immaculate, where they prayed in French and Latin. In his head, the languages mixed and matched, coming together at the Catholic school run by Sister Marie St-Onge, who took the children from both groups and taught below the crucifix. *"Au commencement était la Parole,"* she said, sounding out each syllable, each letter, and waiting for the children to respond. He saw himself standing on a floor of wooden planks, a stove stuck in the middle of the structure built of plywood walls and tar-paper shingles, following the teacher's lessons just as his mother and father commanded. *"Et la Parole était avec Dieu."* He came home and held the book his parents treasured. *"Et la Parole était Dieu."*

The English-speaking workers dubbed the town "Knob" and called the water between Attikamagen and Petitsikapau a lake while Martin's father dismissed it as a pond. Eventually, when Monsignor Lionel Scheffer decided to make the wooden church his official residence, the French came up with the name that stuck. Taken to the airstrip by his parents to greet the monsignor, young Martin hauled himself onto the footboard of a bright red dump truck and looked over the crowd's heads before being scooped up onto his father's shoulders.

He saw men in strange clothes he would later learn were suits and ties. Père Cyr stood in white robes that spread like a tent. Even Marie St-Onge, who called herself an Indian, wore a blue-black dress and shoes that belonged on the wife of a boss. When the plane braked on the runway, Martin still wasn't high enough to get a glimpse of the holy man. The white people applauded and sighed, gasped and shouted greetings, and the Montagnais and Naskapi hunched forward, trying to get a full view from their position off the tarmac. As the monsignor was escorted to one of the few cars in the settlement, Martin finally saw the round-faced holy man with shiny eyeglasses.

The following Sunday almost everyone gathered in front of the wooden church, where Père Cyr had directed the young boys to stand in a V formation that came to a point behind the monsignor. One of the shortest boys, Martin took his place near the crowd, less than three metres from the row of white people. One of the wives winked and waved her bright red fingernails.

Throughout his childhood, he was often called a star pupil and a devout son of the faithful. Père Cyr and Sister Marie marvelled at his ability to read and understand. When he turned seven, they told his parents that their son was the brightest of all the children, a gift from heaven. By nine, he'd mastered multiplication tables and written vivid stories about his relatives who walked into the frozen bush and dragged animals across the snow. He celebrated his thirteenth birthday at the new skating rink and recreation centre. Everyone wanted him on their team; they knew he could score at will or draw out the goalie and pass at the last second. To keep a few games fair, he played goal, laughing at the many times he was caught out of position and watched the puck fly into the nylon net.

After work the miners appeared at the rink, their clothes soiled with brownish-red splotches from scooping or the grey-and-maroon stripes from crushing, a few with the black ovals and ellipses from blasting or greasing. Waiting for their turn on the ice, they leaned on the boards and crowded the gates, cheering and hissing the teenage players. They saw Martin catch opponents from behind as if they moved in slow motion. By the third week, the men had invited him to join their game.

He'd been thrilled, scoring and passing, winning a puck in the corner, racing across the blue line. The men were stronger and better stickhandlers, but they were not as fast. When the game ended around 9:00 p.m., he would towel off his brow and accept a soft drink, then walk through streets half-completed, half-scoured into ice and gravel roadbeds. Crossing the square, he would turn towards the chapel and watch the steeple's silhouette against the blue-black sky or eye the light that flickered in the window of Père Cyr's study. For weeks he thought about walking in the church's side door and up the pine-slatted steps to the priest's quarters.

What would we talk about? he'd ask himself. Unable to answer, he'd move on, heading beyond the pavement and onto a trail rutted by sleds and treaded steam shovels.

On the edge of a trench that supported the rail embankments, space had been made for half a dozen plywood-and-tar-paper shacks with corrugated-metal roofs. Electric wires were strung overhead and zigzagged between them. Martin's family had lived in the fourth one.

The clue came unsolicited as Catherine dodged her family's questions about her personal life. Two young men came through the settlement last week, her uncle said, flashing money and riding new machines. He spotted them in midafternoon and followed their track into town, where they bought liquor and meat. They weren't dragging sleds or equipment from the hunt. Near the station, they met a couple of local Montagnais girls, and the four of them had a party.

That was the first night, which they spent here in Matimekosh, the uncle explained, then they took off for a cabin below Menihek. "They were shooting off their mouths a lot," he said.

Letting the conversation drift to other things, Catherine indirectly rolled it back to the two young men. She inquired about an old friend who'd joined her on many excursions with boys and booze, and her uncle recalled the family, speaking of their decision to leave for one of the reserves near Mignan. To prompt him for the information she wanted, Catherine openly spoke of alcohol and bootleggers, the ease with which they'd always come in and out of Montagnais lives. Her ploy worked.

After deploring the current craze for mixing drugs, for sniffing glue or gas, her uncle mentioned that those two Innu boys were so drunk they couldn't keep track of their gas cans.

"Stolen?" Catherine asked, registering their identity as Innu and trying not to show too much interest.

He nodded. "But they had enough money to buy new ones."

She steered the conversation back to old acquaintances and memories. Though she tried to avoid references to her immediate family, an aunt and a cousin spoke of Catherine's mother and her final illness. The priest, Catherine admitted to them now, had been more help than the physician.

She braced herself, knowing that her uncle wanted to speak about the family and her decision to leave. With the band council administering provincial subsidies, he said he could understand why many left for other territories. A train ride to Sept-Îles and then a bus or even airplane, within two days, a family could be transplanted into a real house, with heat and indoor plumbing; the children could attend better schools.

You left us, his expression told her.

For years, she'd believed that the key to her survival had been her decision to walk away, to let go of the broken clan and mismatched habits of a mother and father straddling life in the bush and life on the machine. Instead of reaching across the chasm between her choices and her uncle's demands, she'd planned on giving his family a small pile of money; she'd taken $1500 from Martin's wad and expected to leave it on their table. But the conversation triggered deep doubts about whether her uncle would accept such a gift. She could not afford to insult her mother's brothers; she'd seen the disappointment in his eyes, his dashed belief that she would return. Without mentioning smuggling or men, he'd let her know that he could see inside and assess her life. As the family's elder, it was his duty to pass judgment — and he did. He could accept her decision to leave and never come back; he could accept band councillors and government handouts; he could even accept the swindles and fast deals in contraband. But he would not countenance her decision to walk away without a family, without children, without any effort to continue their heritage.

So he turned the conversation back to her mother's dying without grandchildren. Catherine required all her control to restrain her anger and hide her pain. It was none of his business; but she also knew her life was his *only* business.

In his sharp stares and silences, he offered a stinging rebuke: you don't belong.

A part of her wanted to fight back quietly, with respect, casting and recasting family tales that would demonstrate her knowledge of the ability of the past to seep into the present. Catherine could tell him of her last days with her mother, the dying woman's dreams and her mournful efforts to let life slip away into the cold, harsh wind of winter. Looking at her uncle, seeing his bitter eyes, she recalled holding her mother's hands, feeding her broth and toast in a green-painted room overlooking the hospital yard in Sept-Îles.

But she said nothing.

She saw that time had taken her farther and farther from this place and its people. Though machines made it easier to cross the barriers that had once seemed insurmountable, the passing of years created new barriers within her family and within the village. The construction of the mine and its town forced the Montagnais and Naskapi to measure hours and days instead of seasons and wind cycles. Catherine had escaped the mines and the band-council economy. She'd manipulated rules imposed by foreigners, but fallen beneath their power and temptations. Martin could flash his cash as a sign of his success; he could buy off many of a family elder's concerns with his money and his reputation as a hunter. But a woman could be only one of two things: loyal, or a traitor who had jumped to the other side.

And therein lay the second problem. As the years progressed, the value of iron ore declined and the mines added up to nothing more than broken promises. After struggling with the machines and the invasion of white labourers, her people were abandoned by the same men and women who'd rushed in and torn up the land, preaching prosperity and redemption.

When she'd returned in previous years, Catherine had been able to face the resentment and envy of her friends, the old-timers who remembered when she ran through the weeded paths that separated white homes from Montagnais cabins, the band-council politicians looking for a fresh approach to land-claim negotiations or grant applications, the young toughs who prowled for glue and hooch. But she had never stared into the angry faces of her relatives, who still believed in Jesus and still remembered the hunt and the feast. In her uncle's anger and scorn, she saw his need to know that his generation's surrender meant something.

But Catherine had nothing to offer except money. To avoid further confrontation, she kept the $1500 in her pocket.

After Catherine told him about the two young Innu, Martin knew where to go. He headed for the rusted rails that angled towards the marshes, walking between a switching yard and a cluster of shacks that once marked the gulley sheltering his father's cabin and others built by Montagnais or Naskapi workers. Though he could see a few lights in the ramshackle buildings, he told himself to resist the urge to take one last look. The cabin was out of his way, and business demanded that he avoid detection.

Nevertheless, he allowed himself one glance. Except for the addition of two structures and the glimmer of galvanized metal siding and braces, the strip looked the same. Despite the darkness, his eyes immediately spotted the fourth house. For a second he was convinced that a gust of wind and snow outlined the silhouettes of his father returning from work, his mother stepping outside to bring in wood for the stove. Maybe he saw his younger brother sliding down the dip on the rusted top of an oil drum.

The gust faded and he turned away from the ravine and followed a loading spur parallel to the old depot. Hooking behind the loading docks, he faced an old drainage ditch that ran towards Knob Lake. With the snow terraced along its angled bank, he broke a path along the sluice to the shacks that local smugglers and deal-makers had used for thirty years.

A new gust of wind brought a cackle from bushes to his right. Then came a high-pitched giggle. He heard a young man's voice and some music. He headed through a break in the snowdrift and approached what appeared to be a group of four teenagers, two males and two females. They were gathered around a fire in a trash barrel. They were passing around a bottle of brandy.

At first the four were suspicious of him.

"I used to live here," Martin said, speaking French. "I did the same thing. But we went down by the water."

They saw that he had raised his hands. "Are you a white man?" asked one of the young men.

"No, a son of the lakes and heights." Martin switched to a Montagnais patois.

The other young man asked, "What do you want?"

"Nothing." Martin paused, then stepped forward. "I'm just passing through."

Now he was close enough to see their faces. He figured the men were in their mid-twenties, the women a year or two younger. The music, Madonna, came from a tape, not a radio station. Judging from the unopened bottles of liquor scattered behind them, Martin wondered if his hosts had begun to understand the rules of piracy and trade. He offered them a pack of cigarettes wrapped in a $20 bill.

"You're here on business?" asked one of the women.

"Yes." He leaned over the fire so they could clearly see his face. "You've been celebrating."

"We've had a party," she replied. "But it's a long winter."

Martin knew how to draw her out. In a calm, deliberate voice, he asked, "Someone gave you an easy chance, eh?"

"They came into town full of money," she answered as the men passed the bottle. "From travelling on the Caniapiscau, they said."

"They bought you a couple of drinks?"

"Yup," replied the taller of the two men. "They really put on some party."

"We didn't plan anything," the girl added. "It just happened."

It took him a while, but Martin figured out the scam. His attackers had come to town with their money, and the women had kept them drinking. At some point, the outsiders were taken to a cabin near Menihek. When they passed out, these two men had come down, stolen eight gas cans, a bit of booze, and disappeared with the women. Then the thieves sold the fuel in Schefferville for brandy and cash, a couple of parts for their machines, keeping some fuel for themselves.

"Anything else beside the gas?" Martin asked.

"Some tools," admitted the tall one.

"They didn't have a lot of gear or food." The other man took back the bottle and passed it to the silent girl. "We didn't want to take their guns."

After she took a drink, Martin asked her, "Did you get their money?"

When it became clear she wasn't going to answer, the taller man spoke. "We left them enough to get back . . . "

"And —" Martin pushed his luck "— that's when you had to take their rifles."

"We didn't want them coming back to kill us!" the shorter man snapped.

"Don't worry, I'm not looking for trouble." Pulling off his glove and reaching into his pocket, Martin brought out a small roll of $100 bills. "Tell me one more thing — where were they headed?"

Each of them took a bill.

"Davis Inlet."

15

Antoine wanted to be the first to arrive. He started three hours before dawn, gathering maps and checking coordinates, monitoring the weather service. It was going to be cloudless and smooth on a route that would immediately take him across the Saguenay at Cap-Trinité. Angling a few degrees south of the commercial routes until the Rivière Manicouagan, he would bank north towards the 1000-metre plateau at Île René Levasseur, then find the old mining pits at Gagnon. At Mount Wright, he'd make the Newfoundland border, then drop into the new airport at Wabush-Labrador City.

He called the tower at Quebec City and registered his path, wanting to avoid the scheduled commuter flights. When the controllers encouraged him to move quickly, he scheduled a departure time before sunrise and packed three days' worth of clothes. From the satchel in the closet, he took four bundles of $2500 and stuffed them in his nylon bag beneath his underwear and socks. Without putting on his parka, he threw the tote over his right shoulder, letting the money rub against the woollen ribbing of his sweater.

At the airport, his red-and-white Piper was the only single-engine being prepped. During fuelling, Antoine walked the length of each wing, his gloved fists firmly knocking on the aluminium, and he listened to the hollow thud that told him ice had not collected in the minus-twenty-degree temperatures. He checked tire pressure, tested the solidity of the landing gear, and worked the back hatch, making sure it would open and close. Then he locked the compartment, knowing it was better to risk a freeze-up than a fluke that would pop the cover in midair.

He moved on to one last batch of paperwork. Unlike a smuggling run to a gravel-and-stone airstrip or an uncharted drop point, this flight was going to be visible and legit. On established commercial routes, there were too many people watching too many radar screens, too many chances of running into the authorities who could bust him for a minor infraction such as failure to file a flight plan.

One of the mechanics stepped up to his shoulder. "You're all set," he said just as Antoine's pen hit the bottom line. "The valves are fine and I gave you a bit of oil."

"How much?" Antoine looked up, then reached into his pants pocket.

The mechanic held up his hand and spread his thumb and forefinger a distance of five centimetres. "Nothing to worry about," he said. "It's not burning oil, just routine for a plane with six or seven years on it."

"Nine," Antoine said, pressing three $20 bills into the mechanic's hand. "Just remember, I appreciate your work. Give one to each of your crew."

"Like I said —" the mechanic paused for emphasis "— don't worry."

Minutes later Antoine submitted his flight plan and checked the large map. The arrows displayed gusts of fifteen to twenty kilometres an hour; he didn't expect any problems.

"How did I get so lucky?" he asked one of the radio men.

"You must have gone to confession."

"No sins," Antoine shot back, heading for the door. "Good conditions for an angel."

"Wabush-Lab City, right?" called a man from behind the wall of maps.

"Yeah."

"Move your ass. The wind'll bring some snow."

"I'll miss it."

He tossed his bag into the cockpit, put on his parka, and climbed aboard. When he finished with the gauges and dials, he plugged in his headset, chatted with the controller, and reconfirmed the weather: clear until noon.

At 5:36 a.m., he headed down the runway.

Madeleine arrived at the train station before the sun crept over the bay at Sept-Îles. She ignored the waiting room and walked into the white-tiled hut behind the station's faded steel-and-glass facade. Holding a plastic cup of coffee, she stood just inside the door and watched conductors and crew gather for the Quebec North Shore and Labrador Railway.

The men swapped newspapers and out-of-date magazines, trading opinions on Leafs and Oilers, Habs and Nordiques, compression and combustion. When they noticed the Indian woman tucked just inside their door, they signalled an offer of muffins. They were used to Indians showing up and quietly waiting for the station to open; the only surprise was that she travelled without children. To them, Madeleine was just another Indian who had journeyed overnight to reach the only regular overland passage from the Gulf of St. Lawrence into the heart of the Labrador peninsula; she wouldn't know about timetables; she'd just come and wait. As long as she remained quiet they could behave as if she wasn't there.

Madeleine was relieved that the rules of this game hadn't changed since her teenage days. She declined a muffin and continued to sip her coffee. She was leaning against the wall and taking up as little space as she could, the overnight bag on the floor between her feet, her purse over her shoulder. She knew they would let her wait here until the ticket window opened.

Martin and Catherine hit the Menihek rapids before sunrise, following the clean-cut grooves created by the many snowmobiles that had motored this way to Labrador City and Wabush. The wind had picked up, but it blew at their backs, allowing them to maintain high speeds without feeling too chilled. Martin reckoned he would have almost three hours' riding before the sun reached the top of the southern skies and its brilliance made travelling in that direction difficult.

When they passed the dam and powerhouse, he calculated they had covered more than forty kilometres in ninety minutes. Slowing down to zigzag onto the route that ran along the railway track, he scanned the western terrace of granite. His eyes found the oblong bowl of red-and-grey stones glimmering beneath the ice, and he gunned the engine.

By 7:15 a.m., the line at the ticket window snaked outside the terminal, women and children spliced between teenagers and single men. Grandmothers, juggling breakfast and bottles, gripped snowsuited babies and toddlers; teens hung in clusters of three and four, knapsacks slung over their shoulders, loud giggles and taunts exchanged between drags on cigarettes. In a patois of Montagnais and French, they talked about school assignments and parents, liaisons in the woods, telephone conversations and MTV, dates, movies, and VCRs. As they approached the window and pulled out crumpled bills for the $36 fare, the teens loudly celebrated school closing for the week of Shrove Tuesday and Ash Wednesday.

Men stood sullen and silent beside duffel bags or valises stuffed with work clothes and outdoor gear; laid-off anglophone miners who found late shifts in the mills or smelters along the Côte du Nord, but could not yet afford to move wives and children; and francophone Montagnais who had stitched together a few days' work on the loading docks, throwing boxes and pushing brooms. Three Naskapi wore new woollen caps and parkas embroidered with the band-council insignia. Judging by their scuffed briefcases, Madeleine figured they had just finished a trip to Quebec or Ottawa, where they were negotiating with bureaucrats.

Ticketed passengers moved down the platform, where pickup trucks, cars, and snowmobiles towing sleds had pulled up near the boxcars. Whites and Montagnais bombarded the blue-jacketed conductors with requests to transport televisions and microwaves, cases of liquor and Pampers, tools and auto parts for relatives in the north. Working at a brisk pace, the conductors set prices, negotiated, counted cash, completed paperwork. Then the cargo was loaded on the first boxcar and receipts were handed over.

The other two boxcars were reserved for larger shipments of lumber, bricks, plasterboard, groceries, machine parts, fuel, furniture, spools of cable, and bundles of pipe. Allocating space and keeping the accounts, a green-uniformed freight agent directed this line of traffic. The half-tons and pickups patiently rolled in and out.

Madeleine settled in her window seat directly across from the heater in the seventh passenger car. She checked her watch when she felt the first tug of movement. It was 8:01.

Antoine picked up the shiny asphalt of Route 389, taking an easy right towards Gagnon, where the empty railbeds were the only signs of the mines that had once broken into 400-metre walls of rock. Swerving east around the reservoir, then coiling north, the blacktop levelled onto the flats beyond Lac Barbel and straightened into Newfoundland — the overland connection between Baie-Comeau, the Hydro-Québec projects along the Manicouagan, and the iron-ore mines in Labrador.

Before the highway was built, Antoine had made regular deliveries of lumber, fuel oil, tools, wire, and small appliances. He'd had a steady clientele of shopkeepers and merchants, small suppliers, and Newfoundlanders or Québécois who held down unionized jobs. But completion of the road in the late 1980s enabled the tractor-trailers to replace Antoine's Piper. Miners spent their income on four-wheel-drive trucks and vans with studded tires to take them down "freedom road" and out of isolation. Less than two months after its opening, during a stop in Wabush to refuel, Antoine saw refrigerator trucks pulling up with tomatoes and apples, oranges and grapefruit, for the co-op grocery store.

"The freedom road gives us a chance to be part of Canada," he was told.

Madeleine gazed at the passing clusters of barren balsam and birch that dotted the Rivière Moisie's eastern bank. When the train bumped and jolted through a sharp bend, the wheels shrieked during a long shift to the left, and she remembered to brace herself for a long climb.

As the ridges tightened and the watercourse contracted, she looked for the outlines of cabins and lodges, the cleared ground of settlement. The train slowed to a gentle roll, and she saw the first switching pole and then the siding. A minute later came the sign: SAUMON. The train curved around the depot, and she spotted the section of water that had failed to freeze, the back-to-back triangular cut her grandfather dared any engineer to overcome. Mis-skat-che-wah, he'd enunciated. The grand rapids.

She traced the switchbacks for five kilometres, watching the riverbed narrow to less than 150 metres. Layered into the corners of each turn were rows and rows of boulders, their grey-green and blue-brown polish piercing the mist rising from the water. Madeleine located the series of paths staggering into the slopes that started at the rapids' southern point and angled east. Mista-kapit-gan, her grandfather had explained. The grand portage.

The paths were chopped through spruce groves and worn into hills of embossed rock, and took a kilometre to rise and break towards the tracks. Then they ran parallel to the train, but split when the fast water darted northwest and the Moisie widened. The tracks, however, forced a hard right into a tunnel heading north. On a ridge flattened by dynamite, the diesel followed a new river, the Nipissis.

Madeleine knew she had another seven or eight hours.

A ntoine left a deposit at the old hangar, then wandered up to the Avis counter in the stone-and-glass terminal. He presented the clerk with a credit card and an Ontario driver's licence, both under the name Robert Desalines, and spoke in English. Confident in the language he had used throughout his years in the military, he exchanged pleasantries with the woman at the counter, watching her slide the card through and punch in his numbers. For $40 a day, the first 100 kilometres free, he found himself behind the wheel of a blue Ford Escort.

He rolled out of the parking lot and turned right onto the icy two-lane road running between Wabush and Labrador City. The midmorning traffic between the mines, shopping centre, rail depot, warehouses, supply depot, loading docks, garage, and offices of the provincial mining regulators was heavy, and he couldn't go more than twenty-five kilometres an hour. But after the dump trucks and heavier pickups took the left-hand fork over a berm that angled away from the switching yard and rail intersection, Antoine picked up speed, crossing the bridge over a frozen canal. On the far side, a sign welcomed guests to the town of Labrador City, Iron Ore Capital of North America.

He went about 400 metres and pulled into the parking lot for the newly built, two-storey, brick-and-concrete Four Seasons

Hotel. He entered the lobby with his nylon bag in one hand and the car keys in the other.

"Almost forty below," he said, stepping up to the desk and greeting the clerk.

"If we're lucky," she shot back in the brogue of Newfoundland. "'Least we have some of the sun."

Antoine was not prepared for her rapid delivery and it took him a moment to understand. "They say till the afternoon."

"Radio tells of a blow from the northwest." She paused to look at the registration forms. "One person, for how long?"

"No." He shook his head. "We need three rooms. I'm the first to arrive."

"You're okay." Her eyes looked into his. "Skiers don't come till next week. Cross-country championships up here at the Menihek Ski Club." She pointed in the direction of the company-constructed recreation complex built between a 1000-metre mountain and a strip of forest that wound around an old mining pit.

"We won't be here that long." He reached into his bag and fingered a bundle of $100 bills. "I'll give you a cash advance."

"That'll be fine."

He put $300 on the counter, then reached for his wallet and pulled out the Ontario driver's licence.

She placed the bills in the cash register. "Might need a little more with taxes, but we can settle up at the end."

"My friends will check in as they arrive," he said as he signed in.

"Of course," she answered. "You'll have a good stay."

Antoine calmly walked up the red-carpeted stairs and entered room 207. A half hour later, he sat in the coffee shop, relieved that he'd established his alias. Without looking at the menu, he ordered eggs and caribou sausage, potatoes, toast, coffee, and juice.

16

The four of them were the last customers in the half-lit restaurant. Ordering large meals so the hotel staff would indulge them with time, they sat in the corner and kept their faces to the shadows, hoping to pass as dark-skinned Canadians or Québécois, not local Indians. They smoothly chatted in French about fictitious families and children, parents or non-existent uncles and aunts as the waitress brought bowls of chowder and small bags of crackers, home-baked white bread, caribou stew, and bottles of warm stout to pour into the cold lager. When addressing the waitress, they spoke English; when discussing the fire and burglary, deliveries and money drop, competitors and Corsicans amongst themselves, they returned to French, never slipping into the Montagnais and Naskapi patois.

The waitress politely inquired about weather in Sept-Îles: Antoine mentioned coming from Cap Rouge, Madeleine from Montreal. When she asked about Martin's trek on the snowmobile, he talked about geology and wind tests, and the routine monitoring along the Caniapiscau that was part of reversing its flow. Between the waitress's comings and goings, they stitched the events together: Catherine provided details of the blaze, her recollection of hearing the snowmobiles, followed by the shock of waking up to the acrid smell of burning tar paper. She spoke of the repeated attempts to re-create what she'd seen through the cabin's window, but each time her memory stalled after a flash of the assailant's blue helmet. When Antoine and Madeleine asked, she described the caribou chase, the trips into the Eaton Canyon and its rim, Lac Cambrien and the Swampy Bay. But she gave no hint of her disagreements with Martin or their frustrations.

Appreciating her restraint, Martin steered the conversation to the break-in at his apartment in Montreal. The way he figured it, the fire was to kill, the burglary to look like a rampage for money; but it was really a search for records of the business that could implicate the Corsicans.

Without giving him details, Madeleine just said the apartment had been tossed. "They wanted to scare me. There was a broken plastic dog in a couple of bags hanging on the doorknob," she said. "They never wanted the money. The bills were scattered all over the floor — around your desk and in front of the bookcases."

"You didn't know the stash was there?" Martin wanted her to talk.

She took a moment to respond. "No. We had a deal, remember?"

He shrugged off her attempt to place him on the defensive. "The terms were simple," he said.

Again Madeleine formulated a careful reply. "I had to keep my nose out of trouble and make sure your apartment was safe. And your part was to get me up here." She paused for emphasis. "That was the deal."

"I remember." His voice was calm. "You must have been scared."

"And confused. I came back to the apartment, opened the door, and the place was a mess."

"Every room?"

"Oh, Martin." She lowered her voice. "Every drawer. And the sofa pillows and chairs were thrown to the other end of the living room. The carpet had been flipped, your bed up-ended, the books tossed out of their shelves all over the floor."

"And that's where you found the cash?" he asked.

She stared into his bitter brown eyes. Her words were a whisper now. "I was afraid I'd made a big mistake somewhere."

His face hardened into a scowl.

Madeleine went on quietly, "I worried I had got too cute. Maybe I dropped a hint during a quick pass. Maybe I played too many angles. Maybe I made all of these mistakes and more. That's what I was thinking."

He focused on her, still scowling. Catherine fidgeted with her spoon, then looked away. Antoine had stopped eating.

In a short, choppy motion, Madeleine slid her plate aside and leaned forward over the table. "I was really worried about screwing you up." She let the words linger. "Can you see that? I didn't know what was going on and I had no way to find out."

"It has nothing to do with you." Martin softened his tone. "You were worried about being trusted."

"I was in the middle. I was supposed to wait for your sign. I'd agreed to that."

"So this happens," he picked up, "and you're caught. You don't know if you led someone to my house. You don't know what you can do to protect your part of the deal."

"That's right."

"You could've run."

Madeleine didn't expect that. It took all her strength to answer. "I tried to stay. My first move was to clean up. I even changed the locks."

"But you still had to run?"

She wanted to scream, but maintained control. "The money is here." She tapped her purse. "I'm not stealing from you."

"That's not the point."

She shook her head. "I don't understand."

"I was never concerned about the money."

"Betrayal, then?"

"Something like that." He paused. "One careless statement, one peek at a few bills — that's all it takes."

"You want to know how they found you?" Asking wasn't as uncomfortable as answering.

He flicked his hand, dismissing her inquiry. "I wanted to know if you gave me away."

"I wouldn't. I wanted to keep my end of the deal."

Martin refused to back down. "Even if I believe you, I still have to worry about mistakes or what might have happened by accident."

She gathered enough strength to press her case. "I was good. As you said, I could've split. Just run away and let this thing play itself out, but I came looking for you with the cash. Do you honestly believe I'd sit here, hand back the money, and then double-cross you?"

"I have to think about that." His mouth twisted in a sly smile.

Madeleine jumped for the opening. "The Corsicans tried to kill you and you thought I would help them. That's what this is about, right?"

"Yes." Martin met her stare. "People can be bought."

Think about it from their position, Martin told himself, settling into the chair beside the bed. As Catherine fell off into the deep sleep caused by beer and a full stomach, he picked apart the puzzle, unravelling his suspicions and fears, piecing together his hunches and the few absolute facts: the Corsicans paid for him to die on the fifth of February, and they must have received a call saying the job was done. They needed to beat the police to his apartment and get lists and dates, times of delivery, inventories and prices — anything that could possibly be tied to them.

When they discovered nothing but cash, they had to assume they were being cheated. But with no leads on his business arrangements, Martin's death became a liability, proof of their inability to control the business. The brothers had to rethink dozens of transactions. After Martin, who moved the merchandise? What was the final price of reaching its destination? When their men came across a drawer of cash, the Corsicans had to consider the possibility that they'd been duped by someone so confident he could leave money neatly stacked in a drawer. Was he a fool? Was he really dead?

So they had to split their efforts to pick up clues. They staked out the apartment and spooked Madeleine, hoping to force her to run; they dangled money in front of Antoine and a bonus if he quietly went over to their side. Like a pro, he went through the motions of defecting. If Antoine had got this far, Martin figured, the brothers had to have given him a chance, while playing the longshot that he'd make a mistake or change his mind.

So that left Madeleine, and they had to watch her. She was unknown. Was she part of the operation, a girlfriend, a relative, a straggler? They would have followed her hustles in the city: the small dope deals and fast tricks, a credit-card scam or a swap of stolen goods. Her moves would've led them only to grifters who had no relationship with one another. The goons must have been confused, watching her dart in and out of traffic.

One question remained: how far did they follow her? To Quebec? To the hotel? Did the hustle for a plane ride throw them off her track? Playing the percentages, Martin reckoned she was not spotted at Sept-Îles and came clean up the railway. Though she acted honourably in the face of compelling reasons to take the cash and run, he still didn't fully trust her. She deserved to be rewarded, protected, but not confided in.

He had to let her go.

"It's the two Innu, isn't it?" Catherine asked, watching him stand at the hotel-room window and stare out at the puffs of white steam billowing from the mines. "You want to get back on their trail."

"I can't stop thinking about them." He paused. "Do you suppose the Corsicans know their men missed?"

"No. They're in Montreal."

"It's the Corsicans I really want," Martin said. "Maybe I shouldn't try."

"First, you're here and they're over there." She stopped to catch his gaze. "They're very well defended, right?"

Martin nodded.

"Second, they're bigger and stronger. They can always hit back." She waited for him to agree. "And third, will it make you richer? Give you more business? What does it accomplish?"

"Personal pride and satisfaction. That's it."

"Could you take over?"

Martin chuckled. "Of course not."

"So this is about you and your territory."

"It's all I have," he replied. "Let's say I find the assholes who torched the cabin, and the message is delivered to the Corsicans. What do I do next?"

She let him answer.

"Do I go back to Montreal and say, 'Okay, boys, let's do business'? Hell, no."

"You think you're finished." She let the words hang.

"I don't know." He put his palms on the windowpane and watched the condensation form their image. "There's only one move — find the attackers and squeeze."

"What can they give?"

"Good question," Martin sighed. "All I know is, they were in the middle."

"So was Madeleine," she countered, bracing for a possible show of anger.

He nodded. "But she didn't have any choice. Once it all started, she was caught."

"And these guys?"

"They attacked."

Catherine remained silent.

"You're worried about your friend Madeleine, aren't you?"

She nodded. "I think she did us right."

"Absolutely." He hesitated. "But this is the trickiest part. If I go up to Davis Inlet after these guys, then no one can hear a word."

"It makes sense —" her gaze fell "— but it doesn't help."

"I can't worry about her," he insisted. "This is more than business."

"Same for me," Catherine replied.

"I still want you to come with me."

"But we won't be hunting caribou, will we?"

"No," Martin conceded.

Antoine studied the orange light creeping over the hills that cradled the iron-ore pits. "I don't like it."

Sitting at the desk, Martin opened the maps. "I just don't see any other way."

"We have two problems, don't we? Getting you there and keeping it quiet."

"That's it." Martin got up and spread the maps across the unmade bed. "If people get the idea I'm flying around, then it won't work. The whole plan is based on secrecy and surprise."

"The whole plan is crazy," Antoine shot back. "There's too much ground to cover this time of year."

Martin leaned over, calculating routes and distances. "I could take the road from here to Goose Bay." He scratched his head thoughtfully. "From there, the trip goes onto the ocean."

"You're talking about a minimum of four or five days travelling in the dead of winter." Antoine shook his head. "That's madness."

Antoine could not let Martin's desire for vengeance cloud his judgment. At this time of year, travel had to be limited and tightly planned: the terrain and weather were bigger threats than any human adversary. It was a simple fact.

But Martin was defiant, insisting he needed this trip to restore what was left of his dignity, to recover his standing. Although Antoine sympathized, he wanted their move to be deliberate, logical, not a suicidal crusade. He knew his plane offered an advantage, but Martin worried it would give away their location; he remained convinced he had to sneak up on his assailants and surprise them the same way they'd surprised him.

"Look," Martin argued, "there's a road to Goose Bay and there's a straight shoot to the coast. You know this."

"You just don't get it, do you?" Antoine shook his head. "You're talking about living outside in the dead of winter."

"I'm going from one town to the next," Martin countered. "The longest legs are from here to Goose Bay, out the inlet to Rigolet."

Antoine's voice hardened. "Why can't I drop you at the airport?"

"Someone would notice."

"Like Madeleine? I can help you and keep an eye on her."

"She has nothing to do with this," Martin replied. "If I fly around, people will figure it out."

"I know you need the element of surprise," Antoine said, crossing to Martin's side. "That's why you have to take Catherine. No one suspects a man and a woman. But I can easily fly you to Goose Bay. It's a busy place. What's one more plane early in the morning?"

"You'll have to register," Martin pointed out.

"So? I arrive at daybreak, pull over to the hangar, let you out, unload the snowmobile and a few supplies. Then I'm gone. By the time I come back here to pick up Madeleine, you're on your way. Who notices?"

"Someone will see you on the log."

"Big deal," Antoine fired back. "Everyone knows I make deliveries and leave all the time. I'm not the risk. The weather is, followed by your stubborn stupidity."

Martin resisted the need to reconsider. Knowing the Corsicans had outmanoeuvred him, he looked for an act of resistance that would allow him to keep his claim to this turf. Though he understood that his assailants were merely young men who were too poor, too desperate, and too ambitious to live a life trapped by band-council rules and welfare payments, his manhood demanded this confrontation; his survival required success. He hungered to prove himself by crossing the peninsula on snowmobile, hopping up the coastal communities, posing as a hunter travelling to the northern caribou herds. With Catherine on the back of his machine, everyone would fall for the ruse. He'd pitch a tent on the edge of each settlement and use cash to buy a few supplies here and there. If needed, he would trade.

"Think about the weather," Antoine continued. "Do you really believe you can make 200 kilometres a day?"

"All downhill to the coast and then the sea." Martin swept his hand over the maps.

"In the open," Antoine reached over and tapped on the blue that designated water. "What about the wind?"

"You have a question for everything, don't you?" Martin cracked a smile and stood up.

"You know it's the biggest trip you've taken in a long time."

"Of course." Martin bit his lip. "There are only a few moves left. I don't want to fuck up my chances."

"We can't fight the Corsicans."

"But I have to do this," Martin countered. "It's the only thing I *can* do. They wanted to kill me on my territory. I can't go away."

"But look at the territory." Antoine jabbed the map with his finger. "Look at the hardships — this town and that town, moving among the Inuit, travelling on the water, the woman. Even if you agree to being dropped at Goose Bay, there are too many chances for something to go wrong. You're not thinking clearly — that's why I don't like it."

"So what's your alternative?"

"Move quickly. Travel light. You know the rules."

"This is a different game. We're not talking about deliveries."

"Doesn't matter. I think I can get you due west of the coast at Davis Inlet. Drop you at dawn and give you the chance to hit the village by nightfall."

The plan surprised Martin, who took a moment to gauge

the distance from Mistastin Lake to the Atlantic coast. "Less than 200 kilometres," he said. "We would cross the plateau and take the Notakwanon River."

"Like you said, all downhill and then the sea."

Martin gave a short laugh. "What about landing?"

"I'd have to go up and check it out."

"It's a beautiful day to fly," Martin quipped. "I'm not convinced, but I'm willing to look."

After the men left, the women settled in the coffee shop. They kept to tea and toast, sipping and nibbling, as clerical workers and engineers and metallurgists wandered in and out. Catherine expected her friend to be tense and confused, but Madeleine apparently saw the clear-eyed logic of their situation.

"This is business, not friendship. It's a deal, right?"

Catherine nodded.

"We're always caught up in one transaction or another. That's always been our story. You don't have to feel bad about this."

"But I do."

"We've always found each other." Madeleine glanced out the window, then back at Catherine. "We go away, but always return. We never really leave, do we?"

"That's what I'm worried about." Catherine smiled ruefully.

"If you stay with Martin and he finds those men," Madeleine said slowly, "you'll have to leave here. No coming back."

"That's the problem, isn't it?"

"Yes," Madeleine replied. "It happens when you mix business and friendship."

17

Martin hunched forward in the copilot's seat, fidgeting with the maps. Focused on identifying a route, he repeatedly checked the numbers of the cockpit compass against those on the maps. Though the numbers pinpointed readings of speed and place, distance and time, the patchwork trail of tree-lined eskers and hills offered sensations of rising and falling, spinning and dipping. From 2000 metres, Martin easily pictured himself crossing these elevations.

"There's no fucking way." Antoine yanked the controls and dipped the wings to the right. "It's nothing but open space down there. Nothing to shield you from the wind."

"I wouldn't cross it from one edge to the other," Martin said, his voice crackling through the headset. "Look at two o'clock. The access road follows the edge to Sail Dykes Lake. From Labrador City to Churchill Falls is an established highway, then I'd take this road. It's half the distance to the coast."

"The hard way is only going to hurt you," Antoine replied.

"There's no glory here. It's simple. You hit and you run. We've done it all our lives."

Martin understood his partner's logic, but he chafed at his own inability to convey the emotion that fuelled his desire. A journey to Davis Inlet and an attempt at retribution would show he would never surrender in the territory that was once his home. He didn't care about the money; he didn't care about the physical risks of travelling in winter. Hardship only added to his achievement. To travel the bush and push his skills was the way. To quietly disappear was a capitulation; to negotiate was a compromise; to overcome the elements, mount a successful strike and escape was the only victory. Antoine's plan offered efficiency, but took away the reward.

"I want to do it on my own," he insisted.

"You're nuts," Antoine replied. "We've used the plane for everything else."

"This isn't everything else. Whether it's done right or not, I won't be able to come back. And if you're involved, well, what then?"

"That decision is already made," Antoine answered. "Our partnership is intact. You'll strike and we're out of here."

Antoine believed that Martin's lust for revenge was rooted in the loss of his business, not the threat on his life. For too many years, they'd faced the risk of attack, understanding that violence was acceptable when bribes and kickbacks, extortion and swindles, proved ineffective. Antoine recognized that the Corsicans had attacked Martin because it was the only way to outhustle him. It was not personal, just a logical extension of their business dealings; after repeatedly forcing the Corsicans to wait and reschedule, rearrange and reorganize deliveries and drop points, he had to pay the price. Though Martin chose to see it as a matter of honour, Antoine wanted to focus on the material issues: together, they had stashed nearly $50,000 that could fund their relocation; he could sell the plane and fatten the kitty; there was money to be collected from Beverly Papineau in Tadoussac, a few accounts to settle with the Mohawks, a couple of lingering deals in Montreal. He may not be able to stop Martin from some sort of reckoning with his assailants, but Antoine wanted to get off the peninsula and discreetly shut down their enterprise.

For eleven years, they'd skipped across the peninsula, delivering cigarettes and liquor, trading fuel oil and supplies, unrestrained by boundaries, governments, and corporations. They'd defied politics, geology, and political economy; they'd broken away without leaving home. They'd entered the white economy, finding prosperity by buying merchandise from the world beyond the Labrador peninsula, but they could only sell to those who remained behind — the Montagnais, the Naskapi, the Innu and Inuit, who could no longer make a living on their own land.

It's just a business deal, Antoine told himself, refusing to turn the events into a struggle for dignity or of principle. A fixed distance had to be covered in a fixed amount of time. From point A to point B. Usually the shortest and most efficient route was a straight line.

"Don't waste yourself," he told Martin. "In the end, we'll still be partners. We'll go some place new and start all over."

"I'm not ready to think about that," Martin said.

"That's the problem."

For the first time Martin openly addressed the need to leave. "We've worked so hard for this business. We didn't have to live behind fences. We were different."

Antoine understood. "You still want to be out there."

Martin nodded, his eyes following the excavated channels that widened above the falls and regulated the water flow. "Once this is done, I'll have to mark a big X through this land —" his voice steadied "— like it never existed."

Working against the brilliant yellow glare of the midmorning light, Martin's eyes checked the shadowed creases made by the windswept moguls of crushed ice and snow. He could not find any remnants of the old Michikamau routes. The reservoir's northeastern quadrant had flattened the ridges and their cracks, stretching them into a glittering collage of crystalline streaks; the backflow had burst through the narrow maze of rock that had once marked the tree line. What had been the height of land, a series of interlocking channels that formed the natural break between Michikamau and the headwaters of the Rivière George, was now a lifeless expanse of dams and dikes. On a winter morning its frozen surfaces sparkled with the sun's sheen; in summer it glimmered with the pale blue reflection of a cloudless sky. But the caribou had crossed into the woodlands along the Caniapiscau, where the reversed river and higher water table thickened the forest with moss and berries, spruce and birch. The fire ruined his hunt. Now the barrens were against him.

"I'm wasting my time, aren't I?" Antoine pushed the throttle forward and accelerated over the black-speckled crest of the esker running east between Lac Romasio on the Quebec side and Gates Lake in Newfoundland. "You're not going to listen."

Surprised by Antoine's bitter tone, Martin said, "I don't think we have to argue. Not after all these years. To me, it's a disagreement."

"Disagreement? This is a lot more than arguing about where to drop and when. This is a lot more than one more deal or a few dollars." Antoine waited a beat. "*Those* were disagreements."

"I thought you'd understand my need to do it this way."

"You know better." Antoine let his anger show. "You don't have to prove anything."

"Only to myself."

"This could kill you." Antoine could not back off. "We have to regroup, not pull apart."

Martin fell silent.

"If you get hurt or stuck," Antoine pressed, "even if I can come and get you, what will you have accomplished? What if you get hurt and they find you? What if someone figures out who you are? Think about that."

"If the Corsicans or my attackers find out —" Martin's tone was flat "— then I'm dead. Plain and simple."

"The object is to get out alive with our money."

"You can worry about the cash. I trust you with it," Martin said. "I'm just asking you to trust me with this."

Antoine sighed. "It's not a matter of trust. Unlike you, I just want to protect ourselves." He glanced quickly at Martin to see if his barb had hit home. Apparently not. "After all these years, that's what I want. A quick getaway when we have the chance."

"Go ahead," Martin said. "We'll always find each other."

Antoine knew it was time to quit. Finally he asked, "Do you want me to keep looking, or should I just turn around and go back?"

"Go back," Martin answered without hesitation. "If you want to help, then let me go. When it's over, I'll come and find you."

"It's going to be very hard to do nothing," Antoine jerked the controls and sent the plane into a wide southerly arc.

Martin took in a deep breath. "You're right about the business. The smart move is to get out with the money."

"For me," Antoine sighed, "it's *just* business."

"Sorry." Martin shook his head and placed a hand on Antoine's shoulder. "I can't agree."

18

Catherine looked at the choices: travel with Martin and break her connection to this territory, or break with Martin and preserve her options. If he succeeded against his attackers, she would be forever bound to him as witness to his actions, participant in his exile. Though she understood that Martin was offering to share his life, this moment was also her chance to walk away.

She could not see herself as a wife, following him to a new location, building his business, protecting his secrets, working on his projects. She'd spent too much of her life avoiding those traps, preferring life on her own terms, even if it meant going back on the run. Martin gave her stability and prosperity, a place to live and a piece of the action, but his determination for vengeance would lock her into his life. In Montreal they had established an equilibrium that allowed her to think her way into his business; she had the flexibility and the skills to be a partner. The city afforded her the comfort of a quick score, a side deal, a few bucks of her own.

But this journey was *his* quest; her presence could be only an extension of his needs. She would play a vital role in camouflaging his intent and setting up the strike, but she would be a weight and a burden. He'd have to cut travel time, change routes, add supplies, think and rethink moves and manoeuvres.

Sitting on the bed they shared, she imagined their conversation. Instead of telling her the truth, he would initially encourage her, insist on his ability to change plans and figure out contingencies. Even if she gave him the benefit of the doubt and believed he just wanted to hold on to her, Catherine still feared his pride, which could deceive him into casting this trip as a redemptive move rather than a bid to regain power over the business.

And when they discussed Madeleine, she grew angry, unable to shake the suspicion he wanted to split the two women and run off with the one of his choice. But Antoine's report of his disagreement with Martin forced Catherine to retreat and reconsider; if he even wanted to break away from his longtime partner, then he wasn't targeting Madeleine.

Antoine's argument had urged Martin to recognize the external perils, but Catherine's focused on the internal danger. Defeat did not faze her — she'd faced many risks to her life and safety — but victory could mean spending her life as Martin's appendage. She wanted him to win, but she didn't want to lose herself to his struggle.

She had the chance to walk away.

During her months in the city, he'd been kind and more than generous. He trusted her and she trusted him. She'd become secure enough to shift from wide-eyed hustler to canny businesswoman, from cute streetwalker to dispassionate calculator and collector. He never flinched from the conflict and craziness, dependence and rebellion, that had pushed and pulled her across Canada and the eastern United States. She didn't scare or intimidate him. So she settled in, accepting his offer to be part of his business in exchange for loyalty and regular hours.

It was more than a job and more than a business deal. Martin gave her the opportunity to live in a different world, to enjoy the pace of a market that thrived on the same contradictions and conditions that had bred her attitudes. Far from the forests and blasted rocks, mining towns and reserves, church schools and hunting shacks, that had shaped their childhood, Martin gave her a sense of belonging.

He embraced her and her cons in an effort to hold on to what he'd lacked for so many years — the feel of home, the fragmented and jagged pieces of life on the Labrador peninsula — and she understood his need to connect with the land that had raised him. He did not have to explain, or quantify or qualify, the frustrations of a life that bridged the city and the bush. She knew that caribou ran in his dreams, as did the drone of a snowmobile and slap of an icy wind. Behind his proud insistence on living outside the territory taken from his ancestors, she felt the heartache of a boy who could not return home.

Though Catherine understood his need for defiance, she did not want to enter a battle that was already lost.

His business was finished. His honour could be measured only in terms of his escape with money. If he wanted to get the Corsicans, she reasoned, then he should show up in their office, give a wave and a quick smile, and never be seen again.

She agreed with Antoine: the smart move was a fast exit. They had enough money to go anywhere; Catherine could still serve as his liaison to the peninsula — make a few runs, keep a couple of deals going. Martin had to know that the odds worked in her favour. If he wanted to keep her, then it was time to expand their partnership, not divide it.

She first laughed at the idea, then repeated it until she felt comfortable.

This was an alternative, she told herself. Yes, she would love to find a compromise that could keep them together.

Martin tossed the idea over for most of the afternoon. The journey would be easier without Catherine. In her eyes, he could see the doubts and fears. He sketched his route on the maps, convinced it was most efficient to follow the roadbeds to Churchill Falls, then motor halfway around the reservoir to Orma Dykes Lake. At that point, he was less than two hours from Marie Lake and the headwaters of the Naskaupi River, where he could piece together the older paths and watercourses that connect the interior to the coast.

With Catherine, he'd have extra weight, extra responsibility. Her initial reluctance would only chip away at his confidence, and that scared him. He knew she could twist his emotions into knots. On the Caniapiscau, he had pushed her beyond restraint, and their muted quarrels had forced him to stop, think and rethink, rearrange, waver, try again, and wonder. This time he had to be in complete control. She would resent it.

It was senseless to drag her across the peninsula.

He wondered whether he could give a time or place for his return. When she mentioned the chance of continuing the business and teaming up with Antoine, Martin allowed for the possibility, but refused the lure. He wanted to concentrate on this journey, on the challenge of food, shelter, mobility. The rest could wait.

When Catherine spoke about money, he cut her off, insisting he didn't want to get rich. He wanted to get even.

He had organized his life around the chance to have the part of his home that could not be taken away by machines, engineers, prospectors, and scientists. The hunt was his — and cash was just a means to that end. He despised the spectacle of helicopters ferrying men from Davis Inlet to hunting camps off the Kenamu River. He had nothing but contempt for land-claims negotiations that gave the band council of Maliotenam the right to run a shopping centre on the outskirts of Sept-Îles. To him these deals could never be fair nor equitable; they were just useful arrangements to move money from one account to another.

This was the point of his business: without going through wholesalers, retailers, taxmen, and truck drivers, he moved goods and exchanged money. He was the main competition to band-council shopping centres and company stores.

And that was how he'd got in trouble. He knew times and places for deliveries and collections, but he did not have enough money to meet the growing demand of his customers. He always had to borrow or order on credit or play the margin, and once he worked with other people's cash, he'd relinquished power. Northeast of Tadoussac, he was the man; only he and Antoine knew that the Corsicans pulled the strings. While Martin kept his accounts straight, he taunted them by jumbling dates, slowing down deliveries, keeping them unaware of who, what, where, and why. He enjoyed needling them. As long as he delivered their money, Martin thought everything would be all right.

Now they'd tried to teach him a lesson on his land.

Martin could not just walk away and give their dollars a victory over his independence. While he understood Antoine's need for a secure business and Catherine's concern for a future, his survival depended on his journey. He would track down his assailants, hurt them, and return to Montreal for one last visit to the Corsicans.

He wanted to get even. Then he could walk away.

"I can't see any other solution."

Catherine took a long swallow of beer and picked at the edge of the label. "It's not going to feel good." She pushed the left corner of her mouth into a smile.

"I thought we were going to fight," he said. "On the way back, after fighting with Antoine in the plane, I thought we were really going to go at it."

"We could have."

"You know it's not the money or the business." He took a swig of his own beer. "The three of you are free to do as you wish. But I need room."

"I don't think it'll work." Her eyes found his. "You'll have to run. Or worse, you'll get hurt."

He waved off that subject and turned to their separation. "We'll have to live with it."

"I thought we could find a compromise." Her gaze didn't waver.

He resisted the temptation to take a long draw of beer and avoid an answer. "There isn't one." He returned her stare.

"I can't wait for you." Catherine watched his hand slide across the table. His fingers crept onto hers, and she did not show her discomfort. "It has nothing to do with using the apartment in Montreal. Or your routes, or Beverly and the Mohawks. That's never been the issue. It's just all these years of moving and drifting, then finally getting a taste of success." She pulled back her hand. "You gave me that. I'll always be grateful. But this trip to Davis Inlet has nothing to do with me. It's not my future, only yours."

He could not hide his disappointment at her unwillingness to wait. "Both of us wanted to fight."

"We tried." She kept her eyes on his face. "I don't know what else we can do."

"What are your plans for tomorrow?" It hurt him to ask.

"Madeleine and I have already spoken with Antoine." She took a breath. "It's all set. We fly out early."

19

In the light snow that swirled in the westerly wind, Martin took inventory. He needed sixty litres of gas to top off his supplies. With 120 litres, he figured on a comfortable week, probably eight or nine days, before refuelling. As for food, he checked the two insulated boxes that held his stock of canned meats and fish, bread, butter, some sweets, a few potatoes. It was enough for one, but he would get some more caribou sausage this afternoon.

The tent and firewood were his big problems. He had to cut tent poles and crossbeams before he left; he also had to carry a pile of logs for fuel — he couldn't risk a last-minute search. To make room for the wood, he cleared a metre-wide aisle down the middle of the sled — food and tools to the left, barrel and stovepipe to the right. The five-metre-long sled could hold twelve, maybe thirteen lengths of spruce, birch, or juniper. He could size the required pieces upon his return.

Before leaving, he grabbed the chain saw, opened the choke,

and yanked the cord. On the eighth pull, the motor sputtered, fumes spitting through the exhaust. He partially closed the choke and pulled twice. The motor kicked over and fizzled; one more pull, and the spark plug fired and the motor geared into a drone. Martin ran the saw for several minutes, putting it through spurts of speed, then letting it idle. Satisfied, he turned it off and secured his load for a two- or three-hour excursion to the woodlands off the southern edge of Shabogamo Lake. No more than fifteen or twenty kilometres each way, he told himself.

Looking for a path out of the hotel parking lot, he turned away from an explosion of wind. He heard the hiss of a car braking, then skidding across the street. It spun left and whipped into a light post; the clang of metal striking metal sliced through the air. While the driver and passengers stepped out to inspect the damage, Martin straddled his snowmobile and hit the starter. As the engine kicked over and he increased the gas, the chain hacked into strips of ice angling out of the parking lot and onto the crusted snow. The machine stuttered forward, picked up the track that served as an alternative to streets, and rushed into the volleys of wind and snow that twirled across Wabush Lake.

Despite the blow and the reduced visibility, Martin was comfortable at twenty-five kilometres an hour. The drag of his sled did not interfere with the turns and curls required to bump around the moguls. He headed for the northeastern shore, where a wooded hill offered a sheltered path, and hooked between the stunted spruce and alder, momentarily losing his vision to a spray of snow. A sharp left and he accelerated up to a patch of flats outlined by rocks and a cluster of spruce. Within three kilometres, he was descending thinly seeded patches of birch and larch alongside a zigzagging esker that dropped to a manmade berm marking the beginning of the railway easement. From there, the path became a bare straight protected by the mounds of earth. When the rails broke east, he took the left fork. In thirty-second spurts of climbing, the snowmobile rushed the forty-degree inclines. Going up required the engine's power; heading down into each ravine required a slalom that taxed his muscles.

He welcomed the exertion. It was a warmup for tomorrow, testing his reflexes and the sled's ability to follow deeply cut turns between brush and bark, stone and gravel. He swerved through the young trees without catching his sled or the slats lashing the trunks. On the flats, he gunned the engine, then used his body to bend the machine into a curve.

When the looping slopes and inclines became switchbacks, Martin recognized the approach to water. He travelled between the fissures along the southern bays of Shabogamo's gnarled shores, looking for the well-rounded cove that arched west. There, the land rose, offering the forested hills that would supply his timber.

He found a four-metre opening in a grove of spruce and parked his machine. Strapping on his snowshoes, he took the saw and climbed the gentle slope. The saw ripped through the bark and sliced into the wood; the tree rocked in the breeze and Martin gave a good shove. When several lay on the ground, he dragged them down the hill and stacked them in order of size on the sled. Then he took off his gloves to thread a rope through the slats and loop it around the pile.

Next, he set off for a birch stand, half a kilometre away. Though often birch retained water and could be difficult to burn, Martin liked its strength for crossbeams, which would be tied to the spruce poles. He pushed through the layer of ice, forcing the web of his snowshoes to snare the hardened granules of snow. He'd expected a harder climb, but the woods levelled out, and he began felling the trees without a hitch.

He now had six trees with enough space for at least six more to be used for firewood. Seeking the dry and brittle juniper, he putt-putted through a wide arch that turned towards Shabogamo's eastern shore. Despite the flat, sandy shoals that were now frozen into waves of snowbanks and iced mounds, he kept a slow, steady pace, peering through the swirl of snow in the hope of spotting the next cluster of growth.

Beyond the first set of rounded hills, where a patch of brown-grey sandstone broke off the lake, he saw the steplike descent that opened to a pond. Visible on the far edge, where the wind cropped the snow into a thin spiral, were the slender barren branches of juniper. He followed the channel to the embankment, then entered the grove and motored to the midpoint. He worked quickly, walking in even, unfettered strides, sizing up each tree and plotting the route of its fall.

He took the long way back to town, picking up the tracks that ran through the middle of Shabogamo and connected to the bend in Wabush Lake. Though he travelled an extra fifteen kilometres, the well-worn grooves offered a smooth ride that never threatened his bulky load. As he passed the crusher, he saw the line of mammoth yellow-orange trucks on six-metre-high tires roll down the access road and take the L-shaped turn into the dumping area. Despite the drone of his engine, he could hear the groan of their diesels and the high-pitched whistles at the plant.

He went through the narrows and slowed his machine, dragging the sled to the hotel parking lot. Eyeing the perimeter for a spot to cut his lumber, he manoeuvred into an indentation that split into a gulley. Once in the trench, he dismounted and refuelled his saw. The juniper were the first to go, easily ripped into thirty to forty-centimetre logs that would be layered onto the sled. Then he turned his attention to cutting three- and five-metre lengths of spruce and birch for the tent poles and frame.

Next, he motored to the co-op grocery and the hardware outlet. With his purchases on the cargo tray built into the back of his seat, he returned to the hotel parking lot, placed the food in the proper containers, and stashed his cache of cigarettes and liquor, extra snowmobile parts, and motor oil. Then he made a trip to the gas station.

By the time he returned, the streetlights were on. He took off his gloves and laced his rope through the eyelets in the edges of each of his tarps. Twisting the plastic layers into a zigzag that allowed him to reach the fuel without undoing the entire cover, he tied and crosstied the twine. He tested the taut surface stretched over his supplies by throwing chunks of ice at it. They bounced off.

With a satisfied nod he went to the restaurant and ordered an early dinner of soup, bread, beef, potatoes, coffee, and pie. Then he went to the front desk, told the clerk he'd be leaving before dawn, and settled his bill. Back in his room, he checked and rechecked his outfit, unfolding the undershirts, turtlenecks, extra leggings, and socks in the muted yellow light of the nightstand lamp. He ran his fingers along seams looking for holes, examining the thickness and probing for threadbare patches. Each garment passed his test.

At last he took a shower and fell into bed.

III

SANGO BAY

20

It was still dark and the temperature stood at thirty-seven below when he left. The forecasters were predicting a slight warming and the likelihood of storms. He hoped to be out of town and beyond the mining loop by daylight. At the curve past the switching yard, he turned onto the railroad easement, taking advantage of the wider grooves cut by the metal-and-concrete stanchions. Instead of navigating the bends between ore pits and roadbeds, he figured it would be easier to leave Lab City-Wabush by taking the constant up and down of straightaways blasted out of the brown-veined anarthocite slabs.

The first flakes fell as he crossed a six-sided tableland pitched over the granular nub of an esker. With the sweep of squalls directly ahead, Martin veered away from the track and took the gravel into a sheltered valley. He could see the ridges opening to a stream that snaked away from the bad weather, eventually leading east through the marshlands that would take him to Lac Ashuanipi. He picked up the trail and held to a speed of about twenty-five kilometres an hour, steadily pushing into the wind.

He aimed for the siding at Ménistouc, where the height of land nudged against the transmission route and the rails. Keeping to the irregular inclines that could jump from a thirty-metre rise to a fifty-metre gulley, he crossed the elevations without difficulty, the chain of his machine firmly powering up the inclines. On occasion, he had to slalom down a sharp ravine or steer into a thinly wooded bluff that interrupted a pointed crust of ice and stone. After a series of zigzagging hills that tipped northwest, he jammed an L-shaped jag to the east, which took him to a set of diamond-shaped ridges. For the first time, he pushed his machine to more than thirty-five kilometres an hour. The gusts of wind jumped over the smooth crests, slapping his helmet and thumping into his parka, hitting left to right, then attacking from the other side.

The speed provided his first opportunity to gauge the security of the sled. The platform swayed with each movement of the steering column. Bobbing, fishtailing, and wiggling, the runners rattled but never broke out of the established trail. On hard turns, the steel-tipped edges dug in and cut grooves into the paths, but on slower, gentle curves, they slid over the bumps and nicks, veering wide of the skis and their drag. To compensate, Martin squeezed the gas, using the flashes of torque to keep his course.

He liked the pace and its challenges, but the work could not completely blot out thoughts of Catherine and their parting, nor of Antoine and the uncertain future of his business. He'd spent years building the network of merchants and suppliers, middlemen and delivery crews, but he knew they could fend for themselves. In Tadoussac, Natashquan, Mignan, or St-Augustin, merchandise now mattered more than individuals. The men and women of these communities had become accustomed to his regular and reliable supply of discounted goods, but now someone else would find the products and transport them. It was the law of the market.

Perhaps Antoine and Catherine, or even Madeleine, would

do it. He'd left them with the opportunity to start their own operation, to earn the dollars to be made from tobacco and liquor. Thinking about their future, however, was an easy distraction that would undermine the purpose of his journey. In his desire for vengeance, he was posturing to preserve a facade even when it declared his friends irrelevant. In all the arguments over this trip, Martin knew what had been most suppressed: his desire for Catherine. He would miss the weight of her body and her lean on each swerve. Her arms had a spot around his rib cage, holding and squeezing. She clutched, he recoiled ever so slightly; her chest came forward, his back stiffened; she tightened her grip, a thrill rolled through him. All those layers of nylon and Gore-Tex, down and wool, flannel and polypropylene, didn't matter; she made her touch known. On the Caniapiscau, they needed each other.

And that was why she had to go. He did not have the courage to accept her presence — and his vulnerability. So he left, determined to face the reality of being alone. On one level Martin had deliberately dragged Antoine into the fray, thinking it would be easier for him to part from Catherine if he showed his belief that his business partnership had run its course. He wanted her to see that he was determined to prove his independence and demonstrate his skills; he didn't want to invest more, knowing the returns would diminish.

Another law of the market, he thought.

It would have been much more comfortable to be angry at Catherine and Antoine, but he denied himself the moral high ground of victim. His colleagues had not betrayed him, nor had they abandoned him. He'd simply defied their wishes and hurled himself into this vast expanse of snow and frozen rocks. He'd told them that this trip was the only way he could leave his home, but the words that rang true in the heat of an argument echoed now as confused and unfocused anger. As he slowed the snowmobile for a series of switchbacks, Martin once again placed himself in the role of renegade, picking his own rebellion to recapture the pride of his youth.

Yes, he was fighting for his idea of home; no, he was not standing on principle.

With this realization, he wanted to believe he had come a very long way, but the landscape did not allow such foolishness. His survival depended on his ability to navigate this one snowbound strip. The room for his mistakes was only as wide as the snowmobile groove.

A t a bend in the rails, where engineers had blasted a circular twenty-five-metre gap through a slab of green-speckled granite, Martin saw the three metallic poles and antennae belonging to spheres of the hydrological equipment that transmitted data to relay points and substations linked to laboratories in Montreal, Ottawa, Quebec, or St. John's. To the right, he saw how the shores of Ménistouc opened to the marshlands heading south for Lac Ocopoca and the headwaters of the Rivière Moisie. That was how his ancestors had travelled to these hills. In the late spring, they began the portage, sloshing through bogs and trekking up the sparsely seeded hummocks and mounds that rose into barren crags of quartz and limestone. Directly below these rocks, where patches of moss formed a scratchy carpet, they turned over their canoes and pitched their tents, and planned their next move.

Martin pulled the snowmobile to a halt beside a line of boulders. Scanning the panorama, he watched the wind bend the outline of triangles into trapezoids and back again. Neither the cold nor the passage of time was his enemy. His surroundings simply demanded that his will had to prevail over his instincts; his journey was a test of stamina, vision, purpose, and desire, not endurance and physical prowess. As a child, Martin was repeatedly told to walk away from this knowledge, but he'd refused. He'd laughed at the Jesuit proposition that devotion and discipline could overcome mountains and bore paths through forests. When the priests began to arrange for his studies in Montreal, he'd teased them with a quote from one of their own: "Almost all of the Indians of New France acknowledge no divinity," wrote the Recollet Superior in 1624, "so material and benighted is their intellect."

Though college was intended to teach him the supremacy of the Lord's word, the city drummed in the power of numbers. There, he learned that the depth of his character was measured in the capacity of drugs or liquor consumed and the size of his bankroll; yet Martin stood on his abilities to withstand the frigid blasts and track caribou. That was why he always came back to hunt.

He followed the ridge eastward for eight kilometres. When he came upon the 150-metre-wide chasm, he stopped, recalling how his teachers had used their maps and books to show that this gap was the trail used by Louis Joliet in mounting his last great expedition. Though Joliet's path went north, then bent west to the headwaters of the Moisie, his father once showed him the elliptical blue-black rock that marked a northeastern passageway. Martin made the turn, knowing he had a straight ride to Ross Bay Junction.

An hour after stopping at the depot, Martin followed the roadbed's ascent through the thickly forested crags. He knew that the Trans-Labrador Highway swerved north by northeast to the bridge at Ossokmanuan Lake. In the four hours of daylight remaining, he wanted to cover another 120 kilometres. Buoyed by the improved visibility and thankful for the gentle slopes created by bulldozers and blasting crews, he held his speed, focusing on the move from one point to the next. Until construction of this unpaved thoroughfare, the terrain pushed overland travellers through the gorge used by Joliet. From there, they could either return to the Moisie or take a long route around the northern watersheds that spiralled to Michickamau and the Grand Falls. Now Martin let himself laugh at his own willingness to embrace comforts proferred by technology. Follow the highway, he told himself. Travel in a direct route and ride 300 fewer kilometres.

The engine's constant rumble and rattle forced his limbs to various exertions. His feet pushed far forward and jammed his boots into the yellow Plexiglas platforms of the chassis, but his ankles and calves had to be loose, not fighting the shaking and grinding of the skis. He had to use his quadraceps and hamstrings to stabilize the machine, squeezing and releasing, then squeezing again, while his arms and shoulders yanked the steering mechanism through a curve. He lowered into a semicrouch to ensure that the 4000 rpm remained centred, pushing down and not rising.

At around forty kilometres an hour, it was all balance and timing, the world a whizzing sequence of grey-white and brown patches with streaks of green and white. While his eyes were directly trained on the snowmobile grooves and ruts cut into the roadbed, he could not separate the stop and go of rocks or grooves that twisted along each side. As he crossed the Rivière-aux-Poissons, he barely noticed the ripple of concave banks that marked the esker. He was surprised by splotches of gravel sprayed into the path and zoomed off the track, the chain spinning without grabbing hold. His arms lifted the nose and he instinctively turned right, forcing the machine into a gulley. To climb back onto the roadbed, he had to gun the engine, nudge upward and rock down, only to hit full throttle again and again.

Martin returned to the grooves and decided to push on, hoping to hit the reservoir system by dark. From there, he could follow the access roads connecting the dikes and dams, relatively flat curves that would take him to the eastern edge of the tree line.

But the Trans-Labrador Highway was merely a prologue to that journey, one without suspense, without excitement. The road made his trek easier and shorter, but drained his sensibilities. The challenges were reduced to pace and reflex; the drone and vibrations of the engine controlled him.

Martin's campsite was tucked beneath a line of stunted alder and half-grown spruce, presenting him with a full view of Ossokmanuan and the frozen channels that swirled around the dikes and dams. He'd pulled off the roadbed within 300 metres of the bridge's first concrete stanchion and followed the flat ridge line until it cracked to a sluice between the trees. Cropped to drain water during the reshaping of the lake and expansion of the basin during the 1970s, the swale offered shelter. Martin stopped his machine and swung his legs over the side, fastened his snowshoes, then stood to bend and stretch.

Uncovering his sled and unravelling the knots that held the posts and beams, he arranged the timber in three piles, then pulled on his gloves to grab the canvas and thicker twine. With the confidence of a man who had performed these tasks many times, he positioned his body as a partial shield from the wind, a move that allowed the fabric to unfold and fall across the mixed layers of ice and snow. He placed the pitching posts around the perimeter and removed his gloves to bind each section of spruce. Then he planted his feet beneath the cloth and hunched forward, his arms hoisting the tent.

In a fast dip and twist, he grabbed the centre pole and drove his heel into the frozen turf, forging a rounded support. Though the breeze flapped and wrinkled the canvas, he was able to secure a triangle. He lashed the braces and crossbeams, and once the tent was standing, he assembled the stove inside. Protected from the wind, he felt the perspiration on his forehead harden into bits of ice that collected in his eyebrows.

When the fire demanded a third and fourth log, he drained his beer and opened two tins of sardines. He skinned and quartered the onion, using the point of his knife to stick each frozen section into the flames. He hacked off pieces of bread with the edge of his hatchet, toasting them to a light brown. He sopped the crust in the salted sardine oil.

Finishing his second beer and three hunks of smoked cheese, he gathered wood for the night, neatly piling the logs between his sleeping bag and the door of the stove.

He promised himself that breakfast would be a real meal.

21

Martin heard footsteps and his eyes popped open. He held his breath and listened, but there was nothing but the patter of ice and snow blowing against the canvas. Rolling towards the stove, he wriggled his torso out of his sleeping bag and reached for a couple of juniper logs. He shoved them into the fire, then dipped two fingers into the jar of kerosene and flicked droplets of liquid on top of the smouldering ash until he heard the *whoosh* of combustion.

It must have been a dream: someone was running at him and he was tied up near a fire. The mental picture recalled his grandfather's tales about Algonkian hunters burned to death by marauding Iroquois, stories of torture and sorcerers, the attacks on the Saguenay, and raids up the Moisie. It seemed as if they'd occurred yesterday. In his grandfather's words, the past was present, here and now, one generation running into the next like a river curling out of rapids. Closing his eyes, Martin could hear the old man's words and feel the fire beneath the soles of his feet, pain streaking past his knees and thighs, then singeing his entire body. Later, when the priest in Schefferville retold these stories as facts sequenced and recorded, he learned that the human voice could alter the passage of time. His teacher's words created progress, one generation moving on from the last.

When he left college for a job in Montreal and came upon the network of Mohawk ironworkers and labourers, Martin initially teased his new friends about their ancestral reputation for war-making by reciting the stories of his elders. The men of Khanawake, he would joke, still carried the aggression that drove the Algonkians to make alliances with Champlain. He'd attribute the church's zeal for conversion to the need to tame the devilish Iroquois temperament. In return, the Mohawks would threaten Martin with the stake, using hot rivets to represent the burning ceremonies made infamous by the Jesuit fathers.

We want you to scream, they would jeer.

His ability to laugh at himself and play this game began the relationships that would create his business and change his life. Instead of walking away from these taunts, he met them head on, with humour and sarcasm, occasionally with debate. His persistence surprised his co-workers; they'd expected him to back down, accept their superiority. Martin conceded that the Mohawks had greater ironworking skills and familiarity with city life, but he refused to give ground on anything else. He was proud of his origins.

Staring into the fire now, Martin tried to sort through these fragmented recollections. Was there a secret, a sequence of events that explained how his life had become a jumbled set of contradictions and paradoxes, half-truths and partial illusions? He wanted to be a smuggler, enjoying the hustles and two-steps that played so many for suckers. For a long time he'd believed that the petty crimes and fast scores avenged the defeat of being born a stranger in his own home. When he started his business, he'd convinced himself that the Mohawks — who'd spent centuries juggling the demands of the French or the British, the Americans or the Canadians — could teach him to apply their lessons to the heart of a peninsula that could no longer rebuff the march of engineers, geologists, provincial nationalists, and international capitalists.

From the Mohawks he learned that a warrior could survive by narrowing his focus and compartmentalizing experiences. If his hands touched the flames, the pain had to be contained in the arm; it could not be allowed to spread. The ironworkers said they did not fear heights because all they saw was the beam and the task at hand.

For so many years, Martin had remained focused on his business and the opportunities it afforded him to move in and out of the land he called home. His ancestors had lived in a relatively stable environment, but the world he knew as a child could no longer exist. In the thirty-nine years of his life, the billion-year-old rocks were unmade and remade; what once moved in circles now moved in lines. In his father's time, these lines had acquired a mathematical logic that could be plotted and graphed, charted and mapped. The land had become a grid of coordinates and magnetic readings that guided airplanes, trains, trucks, and bulldozers into the heart of the peninsula. Vectors and blasting zones became more important than the flow of water. Though the elders insisted that there had to be a divine purpose to these apocalyptic occurrences, the gods remained silent. Believing that straight lines and algebra could somehow relate to Labrador, Martin's father had accepted the white man's god and learned his languages in the hope of finding a line connecting white and Indian worlds.

But the old man was lost when the lines started to curve and angle. The mines in frigid Schefferville closed because they could not compete with mines in tropical Brazil; millions of dollars in Wabush rode up or down with the New York-Toronto-Frankfurt-Tokyo bond markets; climate-controlled computer rooms in Montreal, Quebec City, Boston, Hartford, Washington, or Philadelphia were now wired into the peninsula, where people were still confined behind invisible boundaries created by white men.

For so many years, Martin had believed that the only way to fight back was to jump from line to line, to be a smuggler, to avoid his father's mistakes of becoming trapped in a web of invisible lines.

For so many years, Martin had fooled himself into thinking it was possible.

Halfway across the bridge, he began to see how one piece of the reservoir fit into the next, how the first dikes and dams pushed the edge of Ossokmanuan beyond the marshlands and boulders that once lined the Unknown River. The bulldozers had resculpted the granite into a smooth, oval surface, but the gravel beds retained the outline of erased bends and swerves. From his vantage point, Martin could trace the dotted track of pebbles and shales embedded into a basin designed to hold 100-billion cubic feet of water.

He remembered the original lake, gnarled coves, and islets that converged between a strip of marshland and terraced hills. This craggy watershed, connected to the canoe routes that wound out of the iron-ore crescent at Schefferville, sliced to the south, angling away from the Grand Falls and the streams that drained east into Hamilton Inlet. Though the excavation had rounded many of these edges, he could still see the crests and clefts that marked the beginning of the Rivière Atikonak, where hunters from Natashquan, Mignan, and La Romaine had found their caribou. As a boy, Martin's father said, he'd travelled that way twice, when harsh winters combined with dry summers to parch the barrens and northern woods. They'd crossed the height of land at Lac Brûlé in late August and early September, looking for animals that had drifted east off the Ashuanipi marshlands or north from Lac Magpie. They'd forsaken maps and plotted their location by shifts in the water flow, searching for the smaller streams and ponds that harboured game.

The road flattened on the far side of the Twin Falls power-house, where ploughing equipment and trucks had cleared lanes for the shuttle to Churchill Falls. Though trees still surrounded him, Martin knew he'd entered the reengineered heart of the peninsula, where eighty-eight dikes — not marshes and wooded hummocks, stone crags and barren cliffs — controlled the water elevations between spillways and reservoirs. The K-shaped coves that opened at Flour Lake were now part of the bulbous overflow that had replaced the tight hairpin curves of stone with wide-arching swings of concrete.

He thought of following the old watershed, but instead turned east with the road and steered between the manmade berms and winter-created drifts. The slight turns angled away from the breeze and he took advantage of that, pressing the snowmobile to greater speeds as the skis glided smoothly over the well-groomed trail.

He bypassed Churchill Falls, hooking around the grid of company-owned houses and recreation facilities. He'd come this way as a teenager, visiting his father's work camp and riding a tractor into the construction site. From the top of the diverted falls, he watched trucks rumble down the access roads and deliver parts for the eleven turbines assembled inside a powerhouse built by blasting and clearing more than two billion cubic metres of rock. Overhead, helicopters dragged wire and cable across the gorge, setting up the transmission lines. His father told him that the earth used to tremble from the roar of the falls and its power; Martin could only hear the grating groans of diesel machines clutching into gear.

Now, there was only a constant hum carried inside the wind. The water's movement was manufactured by the opening and closing of 250-ton steel gates installed at a gerrymandered junction of Lobstick and Gabbro lakes. Instead of following the deeply etched channels and rapids that dropped through the grey-black stone, the current was now pushed through 1600 metres of aluminium tunnels. The engineers, by remote control, had transformed the mighty gallop of water into the mechanized production of electricity.

When he stopped the snowmobile and pulled over to assess the intersection of roadbeds, Martin took off his helmet and listened to the *hummmmm*.

The switchbacks and zigzagging inclines took him to the far eastern side of Smallwood Reservoir, and there was no more need for caution: the route opened to straights and tempered turns, leading to the Orma Dykes. With an hour of daylight remaining, he steered off the trail and into the woodland, cutting a trail through an S-shaped hollow that offered protection from the wind and squalls. He reduced his speed to less than fifteen kilometres an hour, spun behind broken circles of sandstone and shale, then stopped.

As he laid out his camp, he began to grasp the full irony of his father's working on the project that flooded his refuge. At first, he merely rejected his old man's choices and decisions as misguided compromises with whites. But as he grew older, Martin began to see that his father had tried to teach him a new way of survival. Instead of passing on the lessons taught to him by elders, he'd made the painful choice of turning over his son's education to the mission. Martin had initially seen this decision as a sellout, then eventually understood that his father had quietly admitted his inability to perform his role as teacher and protector. By encouraging the priests to send Martin to college, he was telling his son to learn more from his classes, not his parents. As a young man, Martin bristled when told that the skills of his grandfather's generation would no longer be needed in the new world of Schefferville and Wabush, Labrador City and Churchill Falls.

In Montreal, Martin came to resent his classes and the well-intentioned whites who talked about culture, hegemony, freedom, and tradition. He resented, too, the academic disciplines that divided knowledge so it could be ordered and managed.

Surrounded by young people filled with the explosive emotions of the FLQ crisis, he found himself restrained by the expectations of his father, who believed that each of his sons would use their learning to secure a better job, a bigger paycheque, a chance of life beyond the mines and hydroelectric dams.

At the time, he'd been convinced that his father had merely surrendered. Now he saw that the old man had slowly been preparing his sons for the dispersal of the family. His father, instead of rooting the clan in its homeland, had seen the bleak future and encouraged his boys to leave. Though his tales and their knowledge of the land's harsh realities would honour their heritage, he'd pressed them to walk into the white world. It was supposed to be a simple deal; he punched the clock to better the lives of his children.

When the prime minister came to open Churchill Falls in 1974, Martin hardened his resolve to reject the rule of whites, learning that his father and hundreds of other labourers had been laid off once the plant was opened. "All these years," he'd said to the old man, "and they don't even have room for you."

His father had said nothing.

22

The warmer temperatures brought a thicker snowfall, which meant a slower pace. Motoring through switchbacks and terraces, shelves that spun into conical hills and forested slopes, Martin followed the slits and furrows of water that rushed eastward. The new powder would eventually help once he reached the wider channels, but he worried about the squalls obscuring his view of any unfrozen patches. If he rode over a soft spot or banked into a granular section, the chain might spin and slip on the loosened particles. He could sink and find himself engulfed by the quicksand-like snow.

Instead of looking for wide open spaces, he wanted to travel in the tight creases of compressed slabs and displaced soil. At ten to fifteen kilometres an hour, the journey did not tax his physical strength, but drew on his mental agility. He had to reason with the surroundings; jagged pieces of rocks could crack a ski; an unfrozen section of river could catch him. Each turn presented choices that required examination and elimination. A right instead of a left might oblige him to make a sequence of swerves and slaloms that landed him thirty kilometres from his goal — the opening of the Naskaupi. With each approach, he looked for the slope, the angle of descent, the drop in a channel, the twist in a ravine as it cradled the bank of silt and ice.

The snow fell faster, the wind slackened, and the ceiling of cloud lowered. He trained his eyes on the green-brown speckles of brush and trees that served as navigational points, then directed the skis towards them. At a clearing that tilted south and bent back towards the northeast, he traced the route by counting the bits of stunted alder that pierced the surface. One, two, three. Connect the dots — and avoid the oval pool of soft ice that opened to a turbulent thirty-five-metre falls, the spray hidden by the precipice that zigzagged behind a line of black-streaked granite. Martin had plenty of time to eye the drop and steer onto the portage carved into a wrinkled face of shale. Pushing the skis onto the only strip of new snow, he barely touched the gas and relied on his shoulders to wrestle with the machine.

The traction held on top, but Martin didn't see the glazed hump of stone at the bottom. When the chain slipped over it, the chassis immediately slid to the left, and he instinctively yanked to the right. Instead of holding their course, the skis rotated and the sled whipped out from behind. Back arched and feet in the air, Martin flipped into a burrow of snow-covered gravel.

He tried to breathe, but couldn't. A moment later, he gasped and lowered his head. After a shallow breath, he rolled over onto his side. His legs moved without pain. Propping himself up on his knees, he saw that the sled had jackknifed and slid into a gulley that elbowed its way between a boulder and a column of granite.

He stood, thankful for the good fortune of only a few bruises confined to his back and shoulders. As he approached the machine and grabbed hold of the steering column, his ability to grip and pull alleviated his fear of cracked ribs. To his surprise, the machine moved; it wasn't wedged.

He straddled the seat and pushed the starter. The spark plug fired and the engine revved as if it wanted to catch and turn over. By the sixth attempt it did. He began a rocking motion that allowed him to jerk the machine and sled into a better angle for creeping out of this contorted position. Then the engine cut out. It took three attempts this time to restart it, and when it held, he jammed his feet into the plastic moulding behind the nose and thumped down on the seat. Then he gunned the engine and the machine lurched forward.

Once on a flat strip of hardened snow, he let the engine idle, stepped off, and settled on his hands and knees to check the skis and steering column. Unable to see any damage, he stood up and moved to the sled. He untied the tarp and looked at the jumbled cargo. Relieved that he only had to face the problem of restacking and rearranging his gear, he eagerly climbed onto the slats, securing the boxes and canisters. The timbers held fast.

He returned to the trail and kept a steady pace until he saw a cluster of mature spruce across a long, skinny ridge. He drew closer to the trees, saw the crack in the rock, and correctly guessed that the gap led to another falls. Convinced that one of these rapids would take him to a riverbed suitable for travel, he took the climb. At the summit, he saw the cascade's spray.

Within two kilometres, he found the bluffs that split into three passageways, and he followed the northern tuck, descending into an L-shaped ravine that banked into the gravel shoals that marked the Naskaupi.

Martin left the river at Wachusk Lake, taking a hard right that placed him on a tributary heading north. He pulled away from the shore and found a forested flat, where he picked up speed, anticipating that the grove would give way to a gentle incline. It did. Next he searched for the saw-toothed gap that curled northeast and opened to the first of three pools. Shielded by spruce and fir, these pear-shaped basins offered him a few kilometres of fresh snow that the breezes barely stirred. Martin increased his speed, cutting a deep, smooth track that gave him enough momentum to clear the shores.

On the far side, he climbed again. As he prepared to swing away from a patch of alder, he spotted the three-pronged tracks of ptarmigans and manoeuvred the machine onto a ledge of stone and ice. Strapping on his snowshoes, he stood, grabbed the shotgun, and sidestepped to the bushes that masked the trail. As he expected, the birds had fluttered for cover. He kept low and leaned into the alder, scanning the larger trees that swung over the notch. If the branches caught a strong gust of wind, Martin reckoned, his prey might shake fee.

He loaded both barrels and waited. The first round sprayed buckshot through the wing of one bird that sprang out of the bough; the second shot blew open the neck of another.

With his haul stashed under the tarp, Martin removed his snowshoes and resumed his travels, finding a campsite on the hills to the east.

By the light of the lantern, he crouched beside the stove and took small sips from a bottle of beer. Yesterday he'd been too tired, his mind too focused on the physical challenges of pulling together his camp. Tonight, he relaxed, his muscles stiff and sore, but his mind unencumbered by the challenges ahead. Now that he'd reached the end of the high ground, he knew that the next phase of the journey hinged on his ability to find the right watercourse to descend to the coast.

Downhill, he told himself. All downhill.

The beer served as a welcome reward for the day's labour. He pulled out two more and considered dinner. Cooking would take time, direct his concentration away from the trip, and force him to operate on a different schedule. After cleaning the ptarmigans, he placed the skillet on top of the stove and let the frozen butter melt. Then he sawed through the frozen potato, bread, and onion. To complement the birds, he added two caribou sausages.

Martin poked and prodded, watching the fat bubble. He dunked the largest piece of bread into the hot grease and took a bite. The garlic and salt, the bits of browned onion, jumped off his tongue as the butter eased the way down. The taste made his mind swing back to the morning of the attack. It had started with his desire to get up and cook a big breakfast. He'd wanted to show Catherine his gratitude for her patience with a life that travelled in six or seven directions at once. On that morning, he'd believed they'd come to a place where business could be forgotten, where he could open this other part of his life to someone who knew the many layered meanings of the hunt and understood the terrain.

His spirit had been alone for so long.

There'd been girlfriends and brief encounters, party nights and lost weekends, a month or two, occasionally a bit longer, but he'd always moved on. Then Catherine came his way and worked. She never expected anything and was grateful for the job. When she brought Madeleine and they showed their abilities, he realized he'd underestimated them — Madeleine was the hustler, but Catherine had the discipline and temperament to think through a deal. At first he tested her, had her do pickups and deliveries, moving stolen goods or exchanging credit cards. Instead of objecting to these routine tasks, she teased him to let him know she was amused by his efforts. She wanted to compete.

That was the attraction. She understood the business and she understood his need to live between the cracks. He saw a hunger for real participation, and bit by bit he cut her in. Though he'd never let the Corsicans know about her presence, he'd had her help arrange the transports and money moves. When she voiced her objections, he listened. He thought of her as a partner.

Working together, they'd collected more than $400,000, and they had the ability, equipment, and contacts to do it again and again. With her help, he could focus on supply and demand, cash and credit. She would take care of the logistics, mapping out drop-off points and delivery routes for Antoine.

Only minutes before the attack that morning, he'd seen their future in the brilliance that broke over the Eaton Canyon — sharp and clear lines running side by side.

But with the attack, his vision had vanished and their future had collapsed. He could not return to his life until he'd stood up to his attackers. He recognized the risk of showing Catherine the part of himself that would never surrender to the common sense that dictated caution. Though it was painful to turn away from her embrace and shelter, he knew he had to make this journey across the peninsula alone. The situation had been whittled down to a choice between his honour and her companionship. Honour won.

The sausages grew plump and the birds softened in the skillet. He separated a piece of ptarmigan, put it on a plate, and began to eat. With the second bite still in his mouth, he opened a beer and leaned back, relishing the lager's chilled carbonation mixed with the bird's heated juices. Only when the bubbles flattened did he let the liquid seep down his throat. He ate slowly, wanting to get the full flavour, deliberately measuring each chunk to be severed and taken out of the pan.

Finally he speared the potato and set it in the skillet to sop up the grease. Satisfied and warmed by his meal, he dressed and stepped outside to check wind direction and speed. The northeasterly squalls brought snow through the cracked rocks and rattled nearby spruce groves. For a moment, he thought of keeping to camp and delaying his journey. Then he shook his head, stepped back inside, and rinsed his skillet with a couple handfuls of snow. The food had given him enough energy to prepare for the morning.

As he settled into his sleeping bag, his thoughts returned to his trek. Downhill, he told himself. All downhill.

23

The trees ended halfway up the foothills that stumbled westward into the Hope Mountains. As the snowfall slackened and the wind gusted from the north, Martin revved the engine, sprinted east across Snegamook Lake and onto the shore. For eight or nine kilometres, he did not have to bank the steering column or twist his body to make hard turns. Now he was on the far side of the Laurentian peneplain, whizzing towards the barrens that descend to the ocean.

It was foreign territory.

He knew he was making progress, but couldn't silence the nagging doubts that questioned each move and decision. He looked at maps, checked his compass, studied the gradients. At any time he could alter his approach, take unexpected turns, replot and recalculate his bearings. Even on these gentle straights, each move could be the wrong one. While he did not second-guess his choice of gunning the engine and bursting to speeds of thirty-five, he understood that his track could lead to a false security.

He had a need for order — a definite location, coordinates and corridors, latitudes and longitudes, accepted standards of assessing distance and time. Reality, however, scattered such devices in the wind that twirled snow and hurled bits of ice. No matter how many times he quantified the machine's pace and tempo, the true measure of his progress remained in the images recorded by his eyes — the landscape flashing by.

On the easy incline to Mistinippi, spruce and larch crowded the base of the hummocks rising to the west of the lake. As the bumps rounded to ellipses and long, fractured arcs, sparse patches of trees gave way to smooth terraces of ice-coated rock, many winding as high as 800 metres. Shoals of granite shard and shale, sandstone pebbles and limestone boulders, punctured the snow and created a checkerboard of barrens along the basin's eastern shore.

Martin remained on the frozen lake, enduring the wind in exchange for a fast run. When the channel connecting Mistinippi to Shapio Lake carved an easterly arc, he momentarily forgot to adjust his steering, and the machine veered towards the hills. Laughing at himself for being lulled into complacency, he corrected his course and pushed onward.

Martin thought of Antoine as he turned into yet another blast of snow. He found himself comparing the new Bombardier's vibrations with those of the aging Piper, and he smiled; this would be a perfect day for Antoine to outmanoeuvre the snow-laden northeasterly breeze. The airplane would dip and dance, bank in and out of the wind, while Antoine searched for the right approach to land on a strip wedged between land and water. Throughout their partnership, Martin knew it was his partner's plane and courage that made it possible to ferry merchandise — to a camp off Lac Péribonca, or the treacherous airstrip built off the channel to Ungava, or the loop over the cliffs at Tadoussac, or the tight swerve at Musquaro that set up the approach at La Romaine. His mastery of flying allowed them to compress time and distance, ignore the boundaries imposed by governments and band councils. In one afternoon, they moved farther than their ancestors did in an entire season. From Betsiamites to Mignan, Sept-Îles to Labrador City, Goose Bay to Kujjuaq, Antoine had constructed their own highway of nations.

And so, Antoine had presented Martin with the chance to service a network of people who thrived in the cracks and crevices, men and women who refused to join the bittersweet sweep of destiny beyond their control. They'd chosen the quick cons and sly hustles of smuggling and black marketeering in a land that had lost its natural order of hunting, tracking, canoeing, and snowshoeing. Flying with Antoine, Martin often felt as if they were travelling through time, not space, generations passed in a few hours of takeoffs and landings.

And as long as governments kept cash only trickling into the reserves, Martin knew their market was secure. Antoine always bristled at the negotiations between buyer and seller, but knew enough to let Martin handle them; he had the talents. One partner understood money; the other airplanes.

That, Martin realized, was what had pulled them apart. The more they travelled, the more they needed the Corsicans. Instead of securing their independence, increased volume and cash flow increased their need for credit arranged in the back room off the boulevard Métropolitain. More cigarettes required more cash up front. The Corsicans exacted their price and pushed for their terms, forcing Martin to juggle deliveries and hustle side deals. Martin's ability to persuade and cajole relied on Antoine's ability to fly and deliver.

At first Martin and Antoine had been seduced by the piles of dollars and the thrill of night flying. Wherever they went on the peninsula, the pair of them had brought mystery and intrigue disguised as power and prestige. As the novelty wore off, however, the stresses had started to show.

Two years ago, Martin and Antoine had come to an agreement: Martin would consolidate and increase the size of the deliveries; instead of repeatedly flying back and forth, Antoine demanded that shipments be rolled out of Montreal to Quebec, then Tadoussac, where he could base the airplane for a week or ten days and ferry the goods. That was why they'd expanded Beverly Papineau's operation to include a warehouse and crew. But the capital came from the Corsicans, and these loans and advances merely placed more pressure on Martin.

Antoine's plane might carry their cigarettes, but it was his own brain, calculations, and cunning, Martin forced himself to acknowledge, that carried their finances. Antoine was happy as long as he just had to handle the flights and ensure that the right shipment made it to the right place. For him, it was easier to take off in a storm or land in a howling crosswind than to negotiate the price or delivery date.

As Martin came to resent the burden of enlarging the profit margin, Antoine shuddered at the slippery double crosses and short cons that became essential to beating the spread. And as Antoine came to realize the amount of money involved, Martin knew that he worried about ruining a good thing, risking the inevitable backlash from becoming too visible. When the two had initially planned this latest huge deal, Antoine predicted that the Corsicans would not allow such leeway with their money. He warned Martin of an attack in Montreal, where the Corsicans, with their control of the streets, would flex their muscles. Martin understood Antoine's fear, but he was determined to show the breadth of his power and skills. In December Antoine's doubts rose again, this time about Catherine, an outsider who had yet to fully prove her trustworthiness and competence. She could blow the whole thing, he warned. When Martin said nothing, both men knew that the limits of their partnership had been reached.

A few days later Martin stretched the Corsicans on their demands for delivery dates and drop-off points and pushed to hold their cash a little longer, a move that would allow him to move more merchandise to different locations and make a few extra thousand. The Corsicans reluctantly agreed, but insisted on getting their money no later than February 15. Martin explained that he would be on the hunt, but Antoine would deliver the cash. Though Antoine had brought the $160,000 to the boulevard Métropolitain with a few days to spare, Martin did not realize at the time that he had finally asked too much of his partner.

As he crossed the tree line now, this knowledge became as certain as the rocks that jutted from the watercourse.

The back of Ugjoktok Bay swallowed the wind and spun it over the rapids that gushed into the northwestern corner. Martin swung around a patch of fast water and found a broad channel, shouldered by black-and-beige-striped slate rock. He had at least two hours of daylight and nothing ahead of him but the wide, flat forearm of a snowbound cove. He could travel past sundown, hit the bulge of land, and motor along the shortcut to Hopedale, where a hotel room and shower awaited. But he knew that Makkovik-Hopedale-Nain formed a circuit for a variety of Inuit travelers — people visiting relatives, moving goods, putting together the hunt, or just moving along to pass the winter months. When he brought merchandise in these communities, he relied on middlemen, who transported the goods in planes and helicopters stationed on the outskirts of the Goose Bay military base. But this time he didn't have these middlemen to give him credibility, and he feared that his appearance in an Inuit town would immediately draw attention. Word of his arrival would move via telephone or radio, or by the snowmobiles that shuttled the seventy-five kilometres between Hopedale and Davis Inlet.

Martin steered away from the sudden, conical jump of granite at that back side of Adlatok Bay, and the land quickly flattened into rectangular ledges and shelves. From the increased strength of the wind, he knew he was only a few kilometres from the ocean and the frigid sweep of the Labrador current that brought the arctic chill down the peninsula's craggy coast. The gusts came from his left as he pulled north and spotted the black-brown clefts that marked the tubular rim of Comma Island.

Entering the 500-metre-wide strait that separated this breakaway slab from the windworn humps and bumps of the continent's edge, Martin stopped at the base of an S-shaped slab of granite. He climbed off the snowmobile and walked up thirty-five metres of iced stone to a crevice that offered a snow-drift surrounded by a broken ring of limestone-and-quartz boulders. After he set up camp, he watched the silver-grey shadows of daylight roll over the barrens.

He splurged that evening, using kerosene to start a fast, hot fire. Spreading his maps on the frozen floor of his tent, he held the lantern, making a wide circle of light on the multicoloured patterns and contour lines. He easily discerned the shape of land and the coastal shoals, then focused on the exact location of the islands, coves, bays, and straits, and he took time to speak aloud and memorize their names and sets of coordinates. Unwilling to distract himself with cooking, he ate out of cans and thought about all the possibilities for tomorrow's travel. When at last he was satisfied he knew enough, he stepped outside to stare at the stars, their luminescence creating streaks of violet across the black sky. To the south sparkled the belt of Orion; to the north glittered the crown of Cepheus.

24

Starting before dawn, Martin could feel his body tingle and tighten beneath the layers of clothing. Muscles grew taut even though the journey — travelling over frozen ocean — had become easier. His shoulders hunched and his stomach knotted as the engine hit top speed. Antoine and Catherine might mock his foolishness and selfish need for vindication, but he could now anticipate the moment of triumph.

He spotted Hopedale against the shadows of rock tumbling into the harbour, the white-painted siding of the Moravian mission glistening across the harbour's south basin. Banking to the east, he raced past the abandoned radar station and the cove that hooked back towards the church with its faded green belfry. Though he couldn't make out the pointer on the bronzed weathervane, he knew that the wind had completed its turn to the northwest, the sign of a clear cold day. The temperature had dipped into the minus forties.

The shoals widened at Anniowaktook Island between the

inner and outer channels that entered the ocean. To gain some protection from the wind, Martin swung back towards the continent, placing himself in the shaft of sunlight that had just crept over the frozen sea. The searing glare off rocks and ice challenged his ability to hold a straight course and keep the skis in their groove.

He drew on his study of maps the night before and matched the smooth surface with a name — Satoarsook Island — completing his mental measurement of distance and gauging his approach. He'd constructed an internal checklist that allowed his mind to order and sequence this portion of the journey. When a two-fingered promontory rose to his left, he immediately knew to swerve towards the sea and circumvent the entrance to Tooktoosner Bay. He waited for the wind to crash against the side of his helmet — proof that he had pulled away from the continent.

When it did, just for a moment, his muscles relaxed.

His tension returned at Umiganiak Island — he'd lost his course. Instead of curving west with the shape of land, he'd followed the light and hadn't immediately realized he was heading out to sea. As the engine tore into the wide open channel, he saw the stark slabs of granite whiz past his right shoulder. He slowed a second later and held his breath — the continent should always be on his left, he knew. He turned and cut a path that arced back towards the cliffs, which the sun made glitter like diamonds.

Relieved to be back on course, he followed the line of crags. As the sun's brilliance increased, so did his desire to see his attackers, these young men who had yet to learn how to walk without a swagger. He imagined their long thin ponytails and sparse strings of facial hair that fell from the corners of their mouths. They were kids who had to be taught a lesson.

Martin wanted to get there.

He'd entered a well-travelled corridor, and he worried that he could lose his advantage of surprise if he came across a hunter or trader. Concerned that someone might recognize him, he accelerated, pushing the engine to full torque despite the rattle and groan.

It was time.

His body shook as he swerved into Blackhead Tickle, where he picked up a snowmobile track and raced northward. Now that he'd come this far, he understood that he had completely left the woodlands and rounded hummocks of his land. He would always be proud of his days as a smuggler, but he knew it was futile to pretend he could hold on to his territory. Besides outmanoeuvring himself, he realized it was impossible to fight the flow of money, which had replaced the peninsula's flow of water. Like his father, who'd helped build the dam that flooded the site of his refuge, Martin had participated in a game that had dealt him out. If he'd remained small-time, if he'd accepted his lot with the Corsicans, he would not be here.

Such humiliation was unacceptable. As he approached the precipitous bluff on the southwestern edge of Napatalik Island, he saw himself stashing his machine and walking through town, quietly tracking his prey. He'd jump from behind, his knife at the throat of one, the other begging for his partner's life, as the sun swung off the ocean into the southern skies.

The jagged bends opened to Flowers Bay, then swirled west to Sango Bay. He pictured the grid, crossing the invisible line that marked fifty-five degrees longitude. Following a yellow-and-grey-speckled slope of quartz and granite, he saw the continent split open and present the strait that would take him to the settlement on the five-sided island in Davis Inlet. He stashed his machine behind the hill that sheltered the village.

Even his schoolhouse lessons had explained how the hunters had spent generations gathering on the continent and trading with the whites who docked on the eastern edge of Sango Bay. But when the closing of the company store cut off a year-round of supply of food and materials, the community was weakened and the elders had to accept a newly built settlement sponsored by the provincial government and the Catholic Church. Instead of anchoring the community on the mainland, however, the bureaucrats moved them to new wood-frame houses built on the sandstone and granite hills that rose from the ocean.

The priests had told young Martin and others that this was progress, but his father shook his head. He explained that the government had chosen the island because it was convenient for delivering the building materials.

A chopper. Cops.
Martin closed his eyes, hearing the shrieks of women.

He fought his panic.

When he was calm enough to open his eyes, he moved uphill a distance, improving his view of the milling crowd. The drone of a second RCMP chopper sent a tremble through his legs.

It was half a kilometre to his machine, and he didn't know what to do. Where could he run?

The chopper touched down, and the people from Goose Bay and St. John's stepped out. The crowd surged towards them, but the Mounties formed a ring around the bureaucrats. Then a few Innu were allowed into the circle.

The band council.

Martin worried that he could draw someone's attention by turning around and climbing over the hill. To keep his cover, he had to go down, even though it would be nearly impossible for him to carry out the attack he'd so desperately wanted. He stepped onto the trail and began the descent, thinking now about gathering information. Perhaps a tidbit, a name if he was really lucky.

Beyond the first row of homes, on a path that led to the company store and the band-council office, he saw another group of people, the women shrieking, the men bellowing threats; they were arguing about the arrival of a liquor shipment a few days earlier. He heard the mention of children, corpses.

He'd come all this way and there was nothing he could do. Nothing, but walk and listen.

From another argument in the doorway of a house, he picked up a snippet about booze and home brew flooding the village. He heard two men talk about gas sniffing. Something about a kid mixing glue or sterno. Someone mentioned kerosene. A woman asked about wiring and the chance to pull the kids out.

Martin rounded a corner and saw a man surrounded by three women. They were striking him with fists and sticks, accusing him of peddling moonshine. As the man raised his forearms to ward off the blows, the women peppered him with claims that his brew was responsible for the fire.

It was Martin's first clue. The accusations shifted: the man had been taking advantage of parents who'd just walked down the hill and wanted a good time, they said. Pointing a finger at the women, the man countered that they had been known to nip from his stock or barter for a bottle of rye hauled in from Goose Bay or Hopedale. Then one of the women stepped directly in front of him and asked how many bottles he'd sold the night before. He denied conducting any business and pushed away from his accusers.

Martin couldn't seem to stop shaking. Tremors stretched from his shoulders to his fingertips. His knees knocked with each step. He wanted to scream, but stayed silent.

There was no chance to escape. The confusion and hysteria of the villagers had engulfed him. To get back to his machine, Martin would have to move against the crowd's momentum towards the village centre, where the mounties and bureaucrats had gathered. Afraid of standing alone, afraid of speaking and revealing his accent, he figured it would be safest for him to get lost in the crowd and wait for a lull.

He threaded his way between groups of men and women, catching fragments of angry conversations. By the time he got within a few metres of the officers, he'd figured out that fire had completely destroyed one of the nearby houses. Through a gap in the crowd, he spotted a heap of ashes and the still-smouldering strips of metal that remained from the wiring and appliances. He heard a man say there'd been a Valentine's Day dance the night before and surmised that celebratory drinking had escalated into a fight and then a torching; a child had been beaten or had caught a bullet, he wasn't sure which, and the foolishness had been elevated into tragedy.

As the crowd pushed him closer to what remained of the house, Martin heard talk of the medical helicopter that had already come and gone; six children had died in the blaze.

For the first time in three days of travelling, he shivered when a gust of wind whipped across his face. The dreary emptiness rattled his body. He'd left Catherine and Antoine and rearranged his life, believing that only in solitude could he recover his honour and dignity and restore his faith in his own abilities.

Though he hadn't considered the possibility of losing their trail or being outnumbered in a confrontation, Martin knew he could have faced such a defeat. But not this. It wasn't supposed to happen this way.

His attackers had come here and celebrated, spread their

bounty, and probably brought a few extra cases of liquor that had found their way to the party. Today the police and provincial officials would have scared them off. Even if they hadn't, Martin knew he didn't dare start nosing around. Too many cops, too many outsiders. No one would trust anyone looking for smugglers and hustlers. Faced with the RCMP and the attention of reporters, social workers, priests, and government workers from St. John's, the community would find its own way to shut out the world and comprehend what had happened. Martin could never make his presence known.

He'd travelled as far as he could and he hadn't got anywere. He'd crossed the peninsula and had nothing to show for it, not even a caribou. To stay here, work through the sequence, and plan a next step required a discipline that he could not muster.

He turned at last to walk back up the hill and heard the cops talk about the need to set up a command post, conduct interviews, and keep a contingent overnight. After they mentioned the imminent arrival of a ski plane, they said parents were to be questioned by the inspector, working in a room beside the band-council office.

It was all over, Martin told himself, holding in a mixture of grief and anger. He summoned all his strength and continued climbing the crest. No one had noticed his arrival, let alone his departure.

Once on his machine, he found the track that swung around the four-cornered point of the land's end. Winding north-north-west between the string of islands and the continent, he told himself not to look back. Instead, he gunned the engine, racing for the granite switchbacks that cut between the blue-and-green-stitched granite cliffs guarding the harbour.

He slowed to putt-putt through the perpendicular drops, then motored to the remains of the village known as Zoar. Dismounting, he strapped on his snowshoes and wandered amongst the ruins. In a shell of cracked clapboard siding and torn asphalt roofing shingles, he hunkered down in a corner and watched the broken windowpane's shadows creep across the planks.

EPILOGUE

Two weeks after the Valentine's Day fire, I met Martin Rouleau in Nain. I was sitting in the far corner of the only bar in town and I watched him slip into the room, wink at the bartender, and follow the wall to my table. He wouldn't sit with his back to the crowd, but positioned his chair so the smoke and half-light would make it difficult for anyone to notice him.

"You're the American who wants to go north?"

I had to laugh at his opening. It was so straightforward and I was so out of place. "Yes."

For an hour, we took measure of each other in wary glances, fast gulps of beer, and bits of conversation pushed through the noise of Inuit men and women. Some were dancing to the music of Madonna, Led Zeppelin, Ice-T, and Bob Marley playing on the jukebox.

When an eerie quiet descended on the room, Martin performed his first act as a guide — he pointed to the television. It was the sports report carried over the cable system that picked up Detroit stations. Though the young men were attentive to the hockey highlights, they erupted at the snippets of a basketball game. With the first dunk, they yelled and hooted for Michael, Scottie, Isaiah, Hakeem the Dream.

Martin was unwilling to fight the clamour, and he brought the conversation to an end. "Wait'll you get to the Kiglapaits and farther — Hebron or Saglek. Then you'll see something."

He told me to meet him at 6:00 a.m.; after checking my gear, we'd take off. Only later did I realize that he'd left without discussing a price.

Our purpose was to hunt caribou on the far side of the Torngats. Pointing to my cross-country skis, Martin spoke of slopes and ridges that would give me enough thrills to fill hours of storytelling in New York.

"That's your book," he said.

We set out, and I thought about the incongruity of journeying into the land of the Inuit with a man who described himself as a half-Montagnais, half-Naskapi trader from Schefferville. As we headed for Port Manvers and motored onto the frozen ocean, I was seized by suspicion and fear: he wouldn't accept my money. I was to help with skinning and hauling animals in exchange for his services as a guide.

I saw myself twisting an ankle in the Kiglapaits. I could topple the snowmobile, upend the sled, break the steering column. He'd have to leave me alone and fetch help.

By the afternoon, however, I was howling with laughter, skiing the groove of his snowmobile up and down the ledge that surrounds the peak at Man O' War. I climbed towards the summit, pushing into the wind, straining to hold stride and keep to the sparkling trail.

We stopped directly below the summit. Martin pointed out our route to the north, the water and stone appearing as smooth surfaces.

An illusion.

Packed in ice crystals that caught glimmers of yellow and orange, a billion-year-old continent was still shaping itself. Blink, and there were shades of royal blue and indigo. Blink again, and the rocks were held together by looping stitches of silver and green.

Nothing moved, but it was always changing.

Fresh caribou tracks appeared beyond the fjord northwest of Saglek Bay.

The sun worked against us, placing a grid of oddly angled shadows on top of the snow; the light shifted from midday brilliance to skewed black lines. In the split seconds between one turn and the next, I watched Martin bobbing and weaving with the rhythm and regularity of a boxer, his head moving with his body, his arms and shoulders directing the machine. There was less distance between hoofprints now; the caribou were moving more slowly.

Martin gained on two grey-brown-and-white stags, looking for any opening through the rocks.

Cornered.

With one knee on the running board, he removed his outer gloves and pumped the cartridges into his .308 Remington. *Clack*. A clear shot at the stag angled between the walls of the crevasse. As he stared into the scope, I counted to myself, "One-one thousand, two-one —"

BOOM!

A burst of blood splashed across the stag's neck. As he twisted and grunted, the other caribou remained frozen in terror. Martin pumped another cartridge. *Clack*.

BOOM! It struck the second stag in the flank.

Clack. He reloaded.

BOOM! Right behind the ear.

I walked to the first caribou on snowshoes, knelt and grabbed its hind quarter, extending the legs and yanking the hoofs. Near the neck, Martin drew his knife and traced a line above the shoulders but beneath the jaw. He paused a second, then began the cut. I turned away, but held the carcass still so Martin wouldn't knick himself. The blood spilled into the snow and hardened. Under the webbing of my shoes were red pebbles of ice.

I didn't see the hatchet until it was hoisted over Martin's head — one, two, three well-placed blows that sent bits of cartilage and bone flying. The head dangled by tendons, which he cut through with the knife.

Then he punched the blade into the animal's rib cage. I had to kneel on the legs, pin them down and pull up on the skin, smooth in my hands. There wasn't any weight, just the cold concentrated in my fingers. I had to focus. I held my scream until metal struck the leg bone. My hands were numb.

For two days, we travelled north, zigzagging between the bare cliffs that dropped into the fjords or the frozen ocean.

A slight turn to maintain balance, and the world rearranged itself. A smooth hump of bluish rock rolled down from the crest, which had to be the magnetic north, but the sun was to the left. Another turn, and the rocks began a gentle decline to rounded hills. Then land came to a gnarled point and ended.

It was Cape Chidley, where the magnetic pull of granite and riptides skew instruments in the effort to pin down coordinates or an exact location. Though scientists have struggled over this conundrum for centuries, the Inuit offer an explanation in the name: Killineq — the edge of all things.

Across a small strait, Martin took me to the Button Islands, smooth and flat, like an afterthought, this grey stone in the frozen sea.

"Draw a line," he said. "Separate the rocks that go west into Quebec from those that go east into Newfoundland."

When I told him it was impossible, he laughed.

"Now you've seen Labrador."

That night, in front of the camp stove, he told me the first fragments of his story.

Over the next two years, in bits and pieces, he described his last major journey as a smuggler. After returning to Montreal in the late spring of 1992, he settled his account with Antoine, taking his $115,000 share of their profits and moving out of the city. He met Catherine on several occasions, but she kept their encounters to a friendly beer or a cup of coffee. Until mid-1994, he dabbled in minor hustles and swindles around Quebec City, Lac St-Jean, and the Gaspé. When it became clear that the government was going to lower its high tax on cigarettes, Martin cashed out with $285,000 and headed for the Northwest Territories.

Antoine, following the advice of his former partner, pulled out around the same time; fortunately he had aggressively pursued his transport business — dropping, delivering, and collecting at a steady pace. He recently settled in western Ontario. "Strictly straight," he says.

Catherine Boulanger took her $115,000 split and enrolled at the University of Montreal, starting with two courses a term. At the end of 1994, she transferred to Laval, just five credits away from a teaching certificate.

Madeleine Rouson invested her money in the cigarette and dope trade. Working out of Montreal, she saw Catherine, but never on business. When the tax policy changed in 1994, she slipped into New York with $200,000 cash. By New Year's Day she was in San Francisco.